# THE DEATH OF A CHILD

# THE DEATH
# OF A CHILD

EDITED BY PETER STANFORD

continuum

**Published by the Continuum International Publishing Group**

The Tower Building     80 Maiden Lane
11 York Road     Suite 704
London SE1 7NX     New York NY 10038

www.continuumbooks.com

Editorial copyright © Peter Stanford, 2011.

The copyright of each essay resides with the author of that essay.

First published 2011

**British Library Cataloguing-in-Publication Data**
A catalogue record for this book is available from the British Library.

ISBN: HB: 978-1-4411-8303-3

Typeset by Newgen Imaging Systems Pvt Ltd, Chennai, India
Printed and bound in Great Britain

# Contents

# Contents

# Editor's Introduction

There is a park bench on Hampstead Heath where I walk the family dog. It is on my regular circuit and however often I stop and read its simple inscription, I am always moved. 'Riley Arthur Paterson Croft, 25 March 2005, lived 35 minutes – loved forever'.

Life, most of us come to learn, has few patterns, few things that we can expect to happen, but most parents still assume that their children will outlive them. For some mothers and fathers, such as Riley's, even that is taking too much for granted. They have to face the tragedy of the death of their child. Each year in the United Kingdom almost 3,000 youngsters between the ages of 1 and 19 die as a result of illness and accident. Every year 1 baby in 100 dies before, at, or soon after birth.

In this collection of a dozen essays, those who have lost a son or daughter tell their stories in the hope that, by doing so, they may help others facing or experiencing the same bereavement. And, that they might afford insight to those of us, among families, friends and loved ones, who watch their suffering, want so fervently to be helpful and supportive, but don't quite know how.

Mothers and fathers are joined in this collection by two siblings who contribute essays on brothers or sisters who have died. They give their perspective, again with the intention that reading their words may support others in similar situations as well as to inform a wider public.

My role as editor has been a backroom one, bringing together the contributors. The credit for what follows belongs entirely to the authors: for their willingness to share something so very personal and intimate in public; for their courage in laying bare the emotional and psychological journey they and their families are still on; for their determination to celebrate the lives, however brief, of children whose futures were taken away; and for their honesty. Some write of how they have been able to go onwards and forwards with their lives after bereavement, others of their continuing struggle to cope with grief.

Each experience shared in this book is unique, but together, at varying lengths, they recall the death of much-loved and much-missed children from the loss of infants through miscarriage and stillbirth, right up to watching a fully-grown daughter with a family of her own die. They also address different circumstances, from physical or mental illness to murder and suicide.

The individual essays are followed by an Afterword on grief from psychologist and writer, Dorothy Rowe. And the collection begins and ends with poems by Seamus Heaney and Michael Rosen, both of whom have experienced the death of a child. A proportion of any royalties raised by this book will go to the Child Bereavement Charity.

Peter Stanford
London, January 2011

# 'Mid-Term Break'

## Seamus Heaney

I sat all morning in the college sick bay
Counting bells knelling classes to a close.
At two o'clock our neighbours drove me home.

In the porch I met my father crying–
He had always taken funerals in his stride–
And Big Jim Evans saying it was a hard blow.

The baby cooed and laughed and rocked the pram
When I came in, and I was embarrassed
By old men standing up to shake my hand

And tell me they were 'sorry for my trouble',
Whispers informed strangers I was the eldest,
Away at school, as my mother held my hand

In hers and coughed out angry tearless sighs.
At ten o'clock the ambulance arrived
With the corpse, stanched and bandaged by the nurses.

Next morning I went up into the room. Snowdrops
And candles soothed the bedside; I saw him
For the first time in six weeks. Paler now,

Wearing a poppy bruise on his left temple,
He lay in the four foot box as in his cot.
No gaudy scars, the bumper knocked him clear.

A four foot box, a foot for every year.

'Mid-Term Break' appears in Death of a Naturalist, Seamus Heaney's award-winning 1966 collection, and in subsequent editions of his collected poems, all published by Faber and Faber. His brother, Christopher, was killed, crossing the road, in 1953 at the age of 3.

CHAPTER ONE

# 'Carrot'
## Carol Drinkwater

*Carol Drinkwater is an award-winning actress whose many roles include that of Helen Herriot in* All Creatures Great and Small. *She is also the author of children's books and a novelist, while her memoirs, based on the olive farm where she lives in the south of France with her husband, have been international best sellers. In 1994, she miscarried a longed-for baby girl, at 21 weeks, whom she knew as Carrot.*

A silent dawn is breaking on a stark, cold morning. The world north of here is blanketed in snow. I am huddled by a crackling log fire. No one else is present at our olive farm, no one except me and our trio of dogs. Soon it will be Christmas. My husband who is in China will have returned. My mother will join us, as well as Vanessa, one of my stepdaughters, one of the twin girls born to my husband and his first wife. Vanessa will be arriving with her three small children. Yes, the upcoming holidays promise a full house; a situation I enjoy greatly . . .

I rarely allow myself to dwell on the past. It is time ill spent. It serves nothing, in my opinion, but just occasionally, particularly during this season of Christmas lights, of family gatherings, the past creeps up on me, throwing up hoary pictures to set me off-balance.

I was in my mid-thirties and newly married to Michel, a French-man I had been living with for close to 3 years. Although I had made my home with him here in the south of France, I still returned regularly to England, still kept a flat in London and still worked as an actress while beginning to build a career as a writer. I was 13 weeks pregnant when the offer came in from the BBC. It was a one-off drama and mine was to be the lead female role. A fine cast was being assembled and the play was challenging. The entire piece was scheduled to be shot on location on the outskirts of Birmingham. The fee would come in handy too, Michel and I agreed, so I accepted the offer.

When Wendy, the costume designer, came to see me at my top floor flat in Kentish Town to 'talk frocks', I deliberated about con-fiding in her my physical condition and eventually decided against it. I had suffered several miscarriages in the past and although this child, this dearly desired little girl, was further advanced than the earlier losses, it seemed wiser to say nothing. I did not want to tempt fate by broadcasting the good news too soon. The BBC shooting schedule was a mere 3 weeks. If I paid attention to my diet, there was no reason why there should be any problem with my costumes.

By this stage, I was a little over 15 weeks into my pregnancy. My energy level was high, diet normal, save for an obsessive craving for tomatoes and no desire for wine, and I was happy. Beaming with joy, in fact. A slight protrusion of my stomach, crescent-bellied, and marginal increase in breast size was all that was visible, and as I am not a skinny bean, have always been described as voluptuous, I saw no reason to concern Wendy or the director. I will have completed my modest part in the shoot before anyone notices, I reasoned.

'God, you look terrif', purred Wendy when she arrived laden with bags and cuts of cloth. She and I had worked together previously on several television films so she knew me a little. 'And so happy. I heard about your new man.'

She had wrapped a spaghetti of measuring tapes about my torso and had begun to jot down figures when the doorbell rang. I was not expecting anybody. In fact, nobody knew I was in town.

'Excuse me', I apologized and hurried to the door to press the antiquated intercom. It was close to 6 in the evening. 'Hello?'
'Flowers for Miss Drinkwater.' The voice was crackly.
The flat was at the very top of a scruffy building with a winding walk-up.
'Flowers?' I repeated, unsure that I had heard correctly.
'Yes.'
'Would you mind bringing them up, please? I am in a meeting.'
'Certainly.'

I popped my head back into the sitting room. Wendy was busy scribbling and sketching in her notebook.
'Sorry about this.'
'Flowers', she grinned. 'Lucky lady.'

I went back out to the landing and waited for the figure, whose steps I could hear plodding upwards from somewhere way below. 'Sorry for the climb', I encouraged. 'It's one floor down from heaven.'

The extravagant bouquet of red roses rounded the spiralling corner before I spotted the delivery man. 'Oh, they are glorious!', and then I was speechless. Standing before me, grinning wickedly, was my husband.

Michel was en route to Australia. Eager to surprise me, he had kept it a *petit secret* that he was changing planes in London with a 5-hour stopover. Instead, he had sped across the capital in a taxi with these magnificent blossoms and a gift to wish me well with the filming, to remind me how very much he loved me, and how very, very proud he was to be the father of our little girl. The gift was a very delicate gold necklace with a tiny emerald set into it. It matched my wedding ring.

Tears sprang to my eyes. I am such a sentimental creature and a gesture as tender, as adoring as this crumpled me. Michel refused to come in, to have a glass of wine. 'Must dash. Plane leaving in three hours', and with that he was gone. From behind a forest of flowers, I watched him disappear down the winding stairwell. The father of my child. 'How romantic is that?!' squealed Wendy when I returned into the living room. 'No wonder you look so splendid.'

The film locations were all situated in and around Birmingham. I was staying with the rest of the cast and crew in a hotel outside the city centre, a rather nondescript establishment where you either crept off to your room and slept or congregated in the bar with other cast members late into the night after a long day on set. It was all part of a world I was very familiar with. I worked hard, long hours, enjoyed what we were shooting and felt no tiredness.

Before the third week, I was given two days off and decided to return to London, to get out of the hotel for a bit and catch up with friends. 'Back Wednesday night, please Carol, without fail. You are first call up on Thursday', warned the ever-vigilant first assistant. I assured him I would be there.

It was that night, or rather in the early hours of the following morning, those witching hours, when I lost our little girl, who for a reason I have never quite understood, I had nicknamed 'Carrot'. I opened my eyes into a heavy sea of semi-consciousness. A dull ache had girdled itself round my lower abdomen. It took me a minute or two to register the fact that all might not be well, that I was damp and sticky. Only when I rolled back the bedclothes did I see that the viscosity was my own blood.

Head swimming, I lifted myself from the mattress and made my way downstairs to the lavatory where it became clear to me that I was losing our baby, ejecting my longed-for little girl. I began to panic. I had to get help. A clock somewhere told me that it was not yet 5 a.m. I was groggy and not sharp or clear in my decision-making and more than anything else I wanted this not to be happening. I called a friend who lived close by in Primrose Hill, waking him, of course, and begging him to come over. He was with me within half an hour.

At the sight of me, Chris insisted we go directly to the emergency department at the Royal Free Hospital in Hampstead. An idea I resisted. I found the home phone number of my gynaecologist who instructed Chris to put me in a taxi and escort me to another hospital in east London where he arranged to meet us.

I was barely able to stand upright, barely able to walk by the time we arrived. Without Chris's support and patience, I would never have negotiated my way through the damp, chilly morning into the emergency area. My specialist was there ahead of us, standing in a raincoat, collar turned up, waiting. His face, always so full of compassion, closed into a frown at the sight of me. He led me into a sulphurous-smelling cubicle, switched on a machine, the obstetric ultrasound, which began to hum happily, and instructed me to strip. Blood, clots of it, was everywhere.

Stupidly I begged, 'We will save her, won't we?'

Only the previous week, Mr . . . , known to me by his christian name, Trevor, had traced out with his finger on the monitor screen Carrot's minuscule bunched limbs, her beating heart, and we had marvelled together at the robust growth of the foetus. She, Carrot, had already become a living, breathing, comprehending person to me; she had become a companion I talked to, confided in. She had become my ally; a travelling companion for the long life that lay ahead for both of us. Plans had been formulated in my mind and transmitted softly to the bulging promise that passed every second with me and had infused me with a joy and sense of satisfaction quite different to any other I had previously known.

Trevor made no response, merely insisted I lie down. The cold head of the ultrasound apparatus caused me to shiver as it slid across the flesh of my naked belly, scanning, homing in on the life of my baby.

'Nothing', murmured the doctor.

'Oh, thank heavens. I feared the worst.'

'I mean there is nothing there. No heart beat, no life, Carol. I am sorry to tell you but the foetus has not survived.'

He might as well have clumped me with a sledge hammer.

'Let's get you directly to the operating theatre and clean you out. We cannot risk infection.'

'I have to be back in Birmingham tomorrow. I'm filming.'

'Out of the question.'

I did not argue. In any case, Trevor was pulling off his jacket, rolling up sleeves, preparing to go to work. Hours passed, lost to me because I was sedated. I still have no memory of the anaesthetist and those hours have remained an abyss. The time it took in surgery to sluice out the remains of my little girl – my dreams of a family, children of my own – I cannot recall any of them. Later, in a private room, I awoke to folk in forest green uniforms wearing facemasks. I was confused but slipped conveniently back into deep sleep. That evening, awakening once more, I found Trevor at my bedside.

'All went well', he encouraged. 'Nothing sinister to report.'

'But is she . . . ?'

'Gone', he replied firmly. 'Get plenty of rest. I want to see you in a few days at my surgery.' He patted me on the arm and then quite unexpectedly, unconventionally, bent forward and kissed me lightly on my forehead. 'I am so sorry, Carol', and with that he was on his way, and I mine, as I descended back into my dark corridors of drugged sleep.

I was not sufficiently strong to travel, and emotionally I was a mixed bag, a knot of anxieties and grief, but the first assistant insisted that I was needed on location. I requested a word with the director who after a hiatus came to the phone, but I could hear he was stressed and needed no problems from the leading lady.

'I have lost a baby', I blurted out.
Silence. Unspoken accusations: *Why the – didn't you tell me you were pregnant?*
'Can you walk?'
'Yes, of course.'
'Then we need you back up here.'

And that was it. I was on the train. Rainy Birmingham. The same grim hotel. At reception I requested my key and to know whether the rest of the team had completed their day's shooting; it was close to 8 p.m. The pale-faced Brummy girl shrugged, 'Couldn't tell yer.'

I nodded and padded off to my room where I expected to find a call sheet with the time that I would be required in make-up the following morning. Nothing. I closed the curtains to create a well of darkness and lay down on the bed.

I had not spoken to Michel and that was uppermost in my mind. His hours in Sydney were the inverse of mine. During my brief stay in the hospital he had left two messages. I had found them when Chris returned me to my flat that very same evening. Yesterday. Was it really only yesterday? I had decided against sharing my loss, our loss, with him at this stage. What could he do, committed to an intense work trip on the other side of the world? Why distress him? I would break it to him when we were together again, face to face. In the meantime, I would soldier on. In a little over a week, I would be back at the farm.

By 11 p.m., I had still not received my call sheet so, sleepless, restless, I decided to telephone the production office at which point I learned that I was not required the following day.

'Oh?'

'We have fallen behind due to bad weather. We'll give you an update tomorrow night.'

Oh.

And so it continued for several days, sitting alone at the hotel, seeing no one, doing nothing but thinking, cogitating, going stir crazy, sinking into a rising whorl of depression.

I had a sex scene to shoot. It was explicit and that was also preying on my mind. To make matters worse, the director and costume director had, during my absence, cooked up an idea, a new costume for the scene: a vulgar black lacy affair, all too revealing for someone as vulnerable as I was at that time. Fortunately, John, the actor playing my lover, was a longstanding friend. We had been at drama school together. When I finally caught up with him, I broke down and confided all. He hugged me tight and promised to take care of the situation, which he did. The black one-piece was ditched. We shot the scene, my last, and I was wrapped. Wrapped, finished, could go home.

Back at the hotel, John and I uncorked a bottle and proceeded to catch up on life. I drank too much and went to pieces. After almost a week of reining in my emotions, I shattered like glass. Other members of the cast arrived. It was not an evening that lives on in my memory as one to be proud of but the three actors in my company that evening were kind, took care of me, and helped me to my room, to sleep.

It was time to go home.

First, a stop in London to see Trevor for a final check-up. It was during this Harley Street appointment that I learned that I was unlikely to ever have a child; that my body for whatever reason was unable to carry an infant to its full term. He hoped that he was wrong, but that was his opinion. I was packed off to see a colleague of his who examined and questioned me. In due course, he promised, I would hear from him by mail.

The months that followed were a very grim time for me. Michel was steadfastly at my side, but the letter, when it arrived, confirmed that due to certain complications, I was unable to bear children, to carry to full term, to give birth.

Childless.

I took it badly and slid into a depression that threatened to engulf me. Somehow, ridiculous as it may seem now on reading this, the idea that I was an actress, a public figure who had been regularly described as 'fulsome', 'sexy', seemed to make my situation all the more unacceptable. I was a woman whom men had desired, but a woman who, when it came to the fundamental role left to play, was incapable, found to be wanting. And I could not get past this point of view, this judgement of myself. I had failed and that was the end of it. My life had lost all meaning, all point.

How did I rise up and crawl from out of that black hole that I had dug for myself? Aside from my husband, who could not have been more caring – but that only made it worse because I believed I had also failed him and the kinder he was, the more profound was my sense of having let him down – nature became my ally. Our farm is an olive farm. Olive trees are eternal – the tree of eternity. They always regenerate.

I began to consider this. We owned 68, 400-year-old trees and were hoping to gain an AOC for the top quality oil our olives produced, but in France to be eligible for such recognition, a holding must carry a minimum of 250 trees. We had intended to plant another 200 young ones. But, in my present frame of mind, I refused to continue with our plans. I wanted no more involvement. I wanted to do nothing. I wanted life to leave me alone, to busy itself in others' worlds, not mine.

Michel suggested we visit a nursery in the Var that had been recommended to us by the AOC offices in Marseille where they propagated AOC-standard olive trees. I stubbornly refused. He coaxed me gently, describing it as nothing more than a day out, and so we made the expedition.

I will never forget the moment when we climbed out of the car with the young gardener who had driven us from their head office to visit the trees. Before me was a sea of growth, an endless silver expanse moving almost imperceptibly in the hot day's very gentle breeze. Beyond, rising up towards a rich cobalt sky, were the mountains of Maures. Purple, aubergine-toned. What a palette of colours, of contrasts, hot and still. Nature, assured of its own magnificence.

'How many saplings here?' I asked of the handsome young man.
He gave me a figure. I have forgotten it. Five hundred thousand saplings, a million, something astounding. Three-year olds, six or nine.
'How many do you need?'
'Two hundred', suggested Michel.
'No, we are not buying, we are only looking. Looking', I insisted but I could not take my eyes away from the trees. Such promise.
'Do you know', continued the gardener, 'here in Provence, we believe that a hundred-year-old olive tree is still a baby.'

'Baby?' I turned my attention towards the young man, such an open-faced healthy fellow.

'These juniors before you are fine examples of the tree of eternity. An olive tree rarely dies and is very hard to kill. Here at this nursery we believe that we are creating the future heritage of Provence. These trees can live forever.'

His poetry stayed with me, gently haunting me, cajoling, nudging me out of my misery even as I shuffled up and down, turning about the hot summer rooms all night, gazing beyond the open doors at the moon spilling its ghostly light over the metallic sea.

In the February of 1956, there was a frost in the south of France and northern Spain that descended to −8°. Inhabitants of Provence who were alive back then still remember it, still talk of it. '*Le Grand Gel*'. The coldest French winter of the twentieth century sparked off an agricultural catastrophe. Right along this coast, from Italy all the way west to the Pyrenees and into Spain, hectare after hectare of olive groves were struck. The exceptional freeze caused the trees' trunk to combust. They were destroyed, or so many of the farmers believed, and they ripped out their ruined trees and replanted their fields with sunflowers or vines.

An olive tree can withstand temperatures of −7° but beneath that they are in trouble. Still, the olive tree is the tree of eternity. It can live forever. It survives.

A few of those farmers, back then, decided to put this philosophy to the test. They chopped the damaged trunks back down to their roots and left their precious stock in the earth. Within a year every one of those trees had regrown. Shoots, small silvery sprouts pushing up out of the gnarled roots that traversed the earth's surface like large grey worms, were bursting into life. The farmers pruned and chose the strongest, leaving those suckers to grow, to flourish. Local history, stories passed down, tell us that all those trees that had not been uprooted survived and today those groves, those 50-year-young regrowths, are thriving and producing fruit and oil.

What had this to do with me, to the crisis I found myself passing through? Regeneration, rebirth was the power I took from this tale and the memory of those lightly argentine saplings growing in the Var waiting to be planted. Up until the loss of 'Carrot', my life here, along this Mediterranean coast, had been blessed. I had discovered love. Love that existed on many levels. Love for a man, for a home, a region, a tree that gave us its liquid gold. The cuisine, the colours and palettes of nature were all about celebration. Until that summer, I had lived this life fully, joyously taking from it all that it offered me, but now I was barren.

Such a horrid, ugly word; such a lonely condition to find oneself in.

Slowly, though, over the months that followed my miscarriage and the news that I was not to bear children, I began to look at life another way. I shifted my perspective. I could give back. We could plant the young trees we had talked of, make our contribution to the future here, and perhaps in years to come, long after I and my private miseries had passed on, others might come to this hillside and find our 'baby' trees, grown tall, ageing into gnarled old masters.

And that was the route I took. We ordered the trees and they arrived in the spring. The Planting Ceremony became a celebration, a form of a christening. Friends descended, placed their chosen junior tree into a hole already dug, drank a glass of champagne with us and the tree was named after them. It was a memorable weekend. Those *oliviers* are now fruiting and we are producing fine oil from them.

I do not consider these young groves to be my children, but I like to believe that I have given back to this hillside a modest offering towards its heritage. My life is not barren. I am not barren. Quite the contrary, I have a very rich existence. Yes, of course, there are moments such as this wintry morning when I fantasize about how it might have been with a family of my own all around me, wrapping gifts for the upcoming holiday, decorating the tree, but then I remind myself that stories unfold in the most unexpected directions and mine has been a surprising journey, full of discoveries, friends, loved ones and myriad paths to follow, unearthed. Barren is the very last adjective I would choose to describe my passage across this earth. Au contraire, I am at peace and count myself very blessed.

# CHAPTER TWO

# *Eoin*

## Catherine Dunne

*Catherine Dunne is an acclaimed Irish novelist. She published her first novel,* In The Beginning, *in 1997, and has followed it with* The Walled Garden, Set in Stone *and, most recently,* Missing Julia. *Her second son, Eoin, was stillborn in 1991.*

Although they are at the other side of the room, I can hear them. The voices are clear, rising without effort over the clamour that has so recently stilled.

'No FH,' I hear the young resident say, dragging her hair back from her forehead. I notice that her fingers are long, her nails shaped and polished. I focus on them, letting her words float somewhere above me. I don't know what they *mean*; but I know what they *mean*. She seems to shimmer, her white coat gleaming in the low light. Everything around me is in layers, etched over a cold, clear blankness. Where the ceiling meets the wall there is a line of shadow. It trembles.

I try to focus on it, to stop it from crumbling.

\*

The ambulance men had wrapped me carefully, as though *I* were the child. They carried me down the stairs, my stairs. Over the threshold. The towels they had packed around me, under me, were soaked through; their heat already seeping into a chill stickiness. Outside, I knew that everything had changed.

*

The silence in the room is now palpable. Someone is still fumbling, painfully, at the crook of my arm. I look down at the top of his head, see the sweat glistening across his forehead. I don't look at the others. Just at him: where pale skin meets the surprising darkness of his hairline. The whole world seems to be composed of light against dark, dark against light. Everything is either one thing or the other. It is itself, or the absence of it. I worry about this.

Then the needle finds a vein, at last. I look up, meeting the gaze of the women in the corner. I am conscious of being watched, feel their eyes underneath my skin, hollowing out my insides. My voice, when I finally speak, is sharp. The spaces between the words are endless and I fall into them, headlong. 'What does it mean?' I ask. 'Tell me what you mean.'

My doctor, Patricia, crosses the room. She takes my free hand. And when I see her eyes, she doesn't need to answer. They fill, over and over. 'It means no foetal heartbeat,' she says. 'I'm so sorry, Catherine.'

I hear her words from a great distance. 'The baby's dead,' I say. It is not a question.

She nods, squeezing my hand. 'Yes.'

I turn away. You knew it, the voice inside me murmurs. You knew it.

*

It is ten to six on the morning of 28 February 1991. As my labour ends and my small son slips quietly – too quietly – into the world,

## Eoin

I learn that the Gulf War is over. It feels that another battle has ended, too. The midwife, Catriona, wraps Eoin in green blankets and hands him to me. The silence is eerie. Last night, in this labour ward, only three babies were delivered. None of them lived. I am surprised, touched and gratified, at how the staff grieves with me.

'He's beautiful,' Catriona says. I reach for him, hold him close, surprised at how warm he is. But of course, he's only minutes old. The cold will come later. I stroke his face. 'Poor little scrap,' I say.

I want a softer material around him; something as tender as the blue blankey that Eamonn, his older brother, still carries with him to bed. This hospital-issue one might irritate his skin.

\*

All that night, we'd held a vigil. Patricia, Catriona, other midwives whose names I no longer remember, and my husband. By turns, each of us wept, laughed, told jokes and stories, moving in and out of sorrow. It was one of those times when significance seems to lurk in everyday objects as common as a teacup. Patricia had been defrosting fat plastic bags throughout the night, warming them in her hands, doing whatever it took to hurry up the process. I became curious.

'What are you doing?'
'Defrosting blood,' she said. She smiled. 'You've used up our supply.'
'Why not put it in the microwave?' I asked.
She laughed. 'That would destroy the antibodies. Don't worry, we're doing fine.'

An abruption, she told me. I'd never even heard of it. The placenta falls away from the wall of the uterus. Abrupt: just like the word. The baby, a tiny spaceman, falls out of his self-contained world, spinning away into a different sort of gravity.

He didn't suffer, she promised. It was just like going to sleep.

Later, much later, I learn of all the ironies. Of the almost non-existent statistical chances for a healthy, well-nourished, non-smoking, socially supported, financially secure, university-educated working mother to suffer an abruption.

Why? I wondered.

Why not, came the answer.

*

We are shopping. Two days later, and already I am walking around the city. My energy brings a whole different layer of meaning to 'new blood'. I am surrounded by the unfamiliar familiar. Buses lurch along. People crowd into department stores, or spill out onto the pavements, clutching bags and parcels. The sky is a bright ache of blue. There are children everywhere, taking up one half of the world.

The other half is made up of pregnant women.

I want to avert my eyes, but I can't. I try to navigate the quicksand of grief that spreads out, treacherously, underneath my feet. And the rage: the hot, visceral, resentful rage.

*

Eamonn has made his choice. His gift for his baby brother. He has replicated, for Eoin, what is most precious in his own small life: his blue blanket. We buy it, wrap it up, head for home. I wonder at this 8-year-old's courage.

'I want to hold his hand,' he'd said, once we'd told him what happened. He looked sturdy, determined. The nurses watched as he unwrapped the green waffle-blanket, took the cold fingers in his. They turned away quietly, coming back later with lemonade, biscuits, a plate of battered fairy-cakes, covered with blue icing and Smarties.

*

People told me it would take time. And it did. But not in the way they meant. Time was stolen from me; it sneaked away, disappearing around corners while I wasn't looking. Days lost their definition, blurring sleepily into nights. Weeks tumbled one into the other, baggy and shapeless. I washed, dressed, cooked, cleaned, drove, ironed, supervised homework and cried.

The one thing I didn't do was look at the still-open suitcase on my bedroom floor. At all those hopeful packets that I hadn't had the chance to take with me to the hospital, so that I might have been able to leave them behind.

Vests, Babygros, nappies.

*

I had never known such restlessness as those early weeks. I walked, paced, fidgeted. Sometimes, I went round and round in endlessly increasing circles. *Round and round the garden, like a teddy bear.*

Round the garden, round the bedroom and, mostly, round the kitchen table. Always coming back to where I'd started, always back to the beginning again: the physical imitating the psychic. You're searching, someone told me. You're searching for the body. It will take time.

Time, indeed. An ancient ritual, all this searching. A throwback to our grieving ancestors, circling the fire, never moving beyond the reaching flicker of its flames. Beyond lay darkness and danger, bodies never to be recovered.

I am compelled to honour this rite of passage. I embrace it, acknowledge that bit of lizard-brain, curled in on itself at the back of my skull.

*

I want to know why formerly kind people cross the street when they see me; why conversation is bright and brittle as glass; why people step around this death as though its shards might make them bleed. I want to know how to answer those who tell me I have 'an angel in heaven' or that I will 'have another one' – as though babies, people, are replaceable.

As I make my way through those early weeks, I long for an outward sign: something to show the world that I am a bereaved mother. I remember the diamonds of dark material, sewn onto my father's sleeve when my grandmother died. I remember how people nodded to him, shook hands, touched his elbow. Strangers and neighbours alike, offered comfort in that small acknowledgement of his loss. I miss that – or something like it.

*

There is a phrase in Urdu which I love. It is 'ghum-khaur'. It means 'grief-eaters' – the community that gathers together to absorb the mourner's sorrow. There are no words in that language for a solitary grieving; no concept of the privacy of loss. No one is ever left to mourn alone. Instead, family, friends, members of the community all protect the bereaved one, closing in, devouring their grief for them so that the burden might be lightened.

*

My first grief-eater was a man called John O'Donoghue, thanatologist. Another word I hadn't known. Guest speaker at a meeting organized by ISANDS, the Irish Stillbirth and Neonatal Death Society, John gave voice to what the audience – so many of us! – was feeling. Guilt; a sense of failure; loss of faith in the future. Pure, blind fury and the need to blame someone – God, doctors, ourselves. Go ahead, he said. Rage away at God, if you believe in Him: He has shoulders big enough to take it. John was forthright, unconventional, sometimes startling – and then he raged at *us*. About the dangers of displacement activities; about allowing our grief to grow out of proportion to our lives; about being consumed by loss, rather than consuming it.

Beware, he warned. Beware the perfect house, where everything is in its place.

That day was 7 weeks after Eoin's birth. I felt the first inkling that recovery was possible. Not just acceptance, not just the ability to 'get on' with things: but the possibility of a full-blooded, whole-hearted reinvestment in life and living.

*

The following morning I wake up, my heart lighter. I crack jokes with Eamonn over breakfast and I see his face blossom. Last night, he'd stood in front of the television screen, his arms extended, hiding pictures of a baby, a box of Pampers. I'd hugged him, hard, told him there was no need to look after me. That was *my* job, looking after him.

*

Then it begins to happen more and more frequently – days, parts of days, even hours that I come to call my 'islands'. These are the times when the storms calm, when peace comes 'dropping slow'. I welcome them. At first, they are no more than opportunities to draw breath, to gather myself, to face the ache of the next onslaught. But gradually, the stillness brings something new and different with it.

I begin to learn how to step from one island to the next, remaking myself as I go. The wastelands in between become easier to bear because now, at last, they are finite spaces.

*

I learn about family, about friendship. About what to ask from each during this long, slow return. I learn, too, that there is no tidy time-table to grieving, no milestones that can be marked off neatly with a tick: been there, done that. It is a process, one that ebbs and flows, that cuts the ground from underneath your feet one day, supports and soothes you the next.

It is a sea of sadness, a river of optimism. It is a reminder of how closely bound to each other we are, how fierce the bonds of love for children.

\*

After perhaps 3 or 4 months, I feel it might help to have some intellectual understanding of what I am learning to manage, day by gradual day. I dive into the work of Elizabeth Kübler Ross, moved by the compassion, the humanity and the honesty I find there. But for me, in the midst of messy emotions that shift and change like light on water, the notion of clearly-marked stages does not resonate.

Denial, anger, bargaining, depression, acceptance: the bereaved should expect all of these *stages*, learn how to move through them. But where did that leave me? I'd had no time for denial. Death had stalked me that night and I knew, even then, that I was lucky to be alive. Anger I'd certainly become acquainted with: and its big sister, white-hot rage. But they kept me company constantly; they did not pass, like ships in the night. It seemed that they would never be finished with me, would never stop winkling out some hurt or other to stoke the blaze of fury. Breasts that still leaked milk; a body that betrayed me by its normality six weeks to the day after I gave birth. And I hadn't had any God to bargain with, either. It was clear on that night that He, whoever he was, held all the chips. What consumed me above all was not depression: it was the acute sadness of separation, of the loss of hopes and dreams.

And then, having to come to terms with the unthinkable: parents are not supposed to die before their children. It's the wrong order.

*Eoin*

\*

There are some accepted standards. Kind people wanted me to know that the first 6 months are the worst; that it gets easier. After the first year, you'll turn the corner. You *will* begin to feel better.

Well, yes and no. If some automatic, linear progression towards recovery existed, then what would explain the presence of all those elderly men and women in the front row of the ISANDS conference? Well into their seventies, they confessed that they had never dealt with the death of their children. Society had greeted their loss with silence, with a refusal to speak the unspeakable.

They had no tools, they said: no knowledge, no understanding, no support. And so they had been consumed by their own private sadness, for decades. There were no grief-eaters for them: no acknowledgement that theirs was a sorrow that demanded to be recognized, shared, softened by talk and tenderness. Recovery remained beyond them, always out of their reach.

\*

Sometime during that first year when the force of grief was at its most unpredictable – felling me at times when I least expected, tripping me up in public, silencing carefully wrought sentences – the wife of a colleague approached me. She looked shy, uncertain. She told me that her baby son, Paul, had died some 10 years earlier. He had been buried quietly, almost furtively: her husband had received a call to turn up at the local cemetery, where he was presented with a small white coffin.

Numbed by grief, blunted by the suddenness of his loss, he interred his stillborn child along with the other 'Holy Angels' – all in unmarked babies' graves. It struck me then how central ritual is to recovery. Without it, we have no starting point, no point of departure, of separation, between the past and the future. We hover in the shadows, unable to move back, unwilling to move forward.

I still believe that the Irish wake is a good institution: it allows for catharsis, for the gathering around of family, friends, neighbours. It is also the reminder of a life that demands to be celebrated: but not before the reality of loss is acknowledged and embraced.

We seem to be programmed to grieve. It is our response to the strength of the ties that bind us. It's a messy, complicated, emotional process, that of absorbing loss and facing life again. With a stillborn baby, there is no past to be mourned – which is another loss in itself – but there are the endless unfulfilled possibilities of the future that we need, somehow, to make our peace with.

And there is a harder truth to be faced here. Although fathers and mothers grieve the loss of their baby together, in reality they often grieve separately. Some say that there is a fundamental difference in relationships that needs to be untangled. That for mothers, the baby's reality has been an immense presence, even if unfelt by others, all through the advancing pregnancy. For fathers, the reality often begins at the moment of birth. There is a disconnect, a skewing of perceptions, a different focus to loss.

For both, it is devastating; but for each, it is different.

*

The comfort of ritual; the company of grief-eaters; learning to live from one moment to the next; valuing the power of spoken and written words: all of this got me through. It's hard to chart recovery, in the same way that it is impossible to grieve in stages.

But a guesstimate of 4 years is as good as any. At that point, grief ceased to ambush me. It moved to a different register; it acquired a new tone; it came from a different place: a place where consciousness of loss was overlaid by an engagement with the present. For me, a strong sense of having been 'spared' eventually began to grow.

*Eoin*

It was accompanied at the same time by a dark surge of guilt – how come *I* was the one to survive, and not my son? Survivor guilt, before I'd ever heard the term. But this sense of having been given another chance became stronger and stronger in the next few years. It began to feel, truly, like a gift.

What are you going to do now, a friend asked, with your one wild and wonderful life?

What I've always wanted, that's what.

*

I began to write like a demon, once the Arctic wastes of grief began to thaw. Blankness receded. I could focus again, sleep again, celebrate the birth of other people's babies again. The world no longer showed itself to me in black and white. It was now peopled with more subtle colours, more shade than shadow. The shoots of recovery that I had once sensed were becoming hardy plants; still susceptible to frost, but nonetheless, strongly rooted in the future.

And writing made me.

It allowed me to inhabit another universe; it made me feel at home, rather than dislocated by loss; it allowed me to experience the transformative power of fiction. And by so doing, it allowed me to transform myself.

*

Eoin is still part of my daily life. No longer the blinding light in the middle of my forehead that obscures everything else, he nevertheless abides with me. A gentle presence, an exacting taskmaster. He has taught me that grief is, above all, a sense of separation so acute that even now, 20 years later, I can access it with no difficulty at all, and not a little emotion.

*

Would I wish it different? Of course I would. He'd be approaching his twentieth birthday now, and I often imagine him at my table. He has his own decoration on my Christmas tree, his own place wherever I am.

But it is a place that is appropriate to the rest of my life.

John O'Donoghue likened the early days of grief to a huge photograph in the house, a picture of the dead baby that dominates the mantelpiece, the room, the lives of all who live there. Gradually, the image needs to become smaller: still there, but no longer overwhelming.

It has taken time – time that was no longer stolen, but used, properly, in order to gain a foothold in the underworld of grieving.

Now, Eoin is of passport size, so that I can take him with me wherever I go. My travelling companion; my son; my teacher. I can't help wondering what he'd look like. When I do, I just look at his brother.

And I smile.

CHAPTER THREE

# *Jennifer*
### Sarah Brown

*Sarah Brown is the founder of PiggyBankKids which works on a range of charitable projects changing lives of babies and children. She and her husband, former UK Prime Minister, Gordon Brown, have two sons. Their daughter Jennifer, died in 2002 at 10 days old.*

There is surely nothing worse than losing your much-loved child. Nothing at all.

Every day I remember our daughter Jennifer and cherish the 10 days we were able to spend with her.

Every day I try to focus on the happy memories that exist as a way to remember and appreciate her short life.

Every day I hope also to help the impact of her life grow through the life-saving work of scientists at the Jennifer Brown Research Laboratory in Edinburgh. Their clinical work on the causes and consequences of pregnancy difficulties and prematurity is ground-breaking. The research team is doggedly looking for new information to help the work of our great obstetricians, midwives and other professionals across the Health Service. We have the support of many other parents who make a little sense of their own loss through seeking to help other babies and families in the future.

In the United Kingdom about 1 in 200 babies dies soon after birth from pregnancy, delivery and other complications. In addition, about 1 in 200 stillbirths means further loss and anguish for parents. Of course, in the developing world where the rate of infant and maternal mortality is so high, the tragedy of each loss is equally great, but more commonplace, and many of those deaths so heartbreakingly preventable with simple interventions.

Since Jennifer's death in 2002, I have spoken many times to mums and dads, grandparents, other family members and close friends who have experienced a similar loss. We all learn from each other. There is lots of advice to be had, of course, but everyone has their personal journey to take. Talking with others is so valuable. And the cliché that the passage of time helps is certainly true. The first lesson is to recognize that the big overwhelming debilitating pain that hits from time to time does subside and, as hard as it is to go through it, you learn that you do come out of the other side each time.

The advice that most helped me is something I don't even remember whether I was told personally or read in a book, but it made all the difference. I learned simply that I did not need to find a way to mend myself, nor to return to being the person I was before. I had assumed that I must find a way to recover and resume my life which proved impossible. Instead I realized that the loss of Jennifer had changed me forever, and importantly I realized that this was okay. With that understanding, a burden lifted from my shoulders and I looked afresh at how to move forward. I see others struggle to resume their familiar lives and often share that piece of advice.

The other thing I have learned is to continually open my heart to the love I feel for my daughter, no matter how painful that can be at times. There is a temptation to put something that hurts to one side in order to cope better in daily life. Actually the reverse is true. Just recognizing the full extent of your love means you can cherish, remember and properly honour the person you have lost – and know that you are denying them nothing. As all parents know, your child is the first person you meet for whom you would do anything at all, with no thought for your own self.

It is as true for the child who lives in your heart as for the child who lives in your home.

# CHAPTER FOUR

# *Clare*

### Joanna Moorhead

*Joanna Moorhead is an award-winning journalist who writes on social and health issues for the* Guardian, *the* Independent *and many other papers and magazines. She has also curated an exhibition of work by her cousin, the surrealist painter, Leonora Carrington. Her sister, Clare, died in 1972 at the age of 3.*

It happened on a perfect summer's day; a day when the sun poured down from a faultlessly blue sky. All that morning, we children played under that sky. We ran around the garden; we rode on our bicycles; we splashed in our paddling pool. If you had happened to glimpse us, over our neighbour's fence perhaps, you would have thought we were four very lucky, and very happy, young children indeed; and at that precise moment, we undoubtedly *were* among the luckiest, and maybe happiest, children imaginable.

But our world was about to become very unlucky, and our happiness was about to be stolen away; because what we were doing that morning, though we had no inkling of it, was playing out the final hours of our childhood. For one of us in the garden that day, these were to be the last few hours of any kind of life at all. For the other three, they were the final hours before we would be horribly wounded: not physically wounded, as our sister would be, but psychologically wounded. And those psychological scars would be ones we'd carry, through the rest of our lives.

And all of this was happening under a cloudless, perfect sky. Ever since, I have never trusted a summer's day again. After all, that day taught me the truth: which is that, however safe and warm and bright and happy a sunny day might be, it can all be swept away in seconds. And if it is, nothing will ever be the same again.

The day I am remembering was 19 July 1972. The weather, as I say, was perfect: it was one of those endless, school holiday days, the kind of day when children like us spent our entire day outside, playing in the garden, going to call on friends nearby, and wandering back and forth between their houses and our own. I was not quite 10 at the time; my next sister was 8, and my brother had just turned 6. Clare, our youngest sister, was 3 months away from her fourth birthday.

I played with Clare for a while that morning, in the garden: and then I decided to wander down the road to see a friend. As one of the older children, I was allowed to walk round the neighbourhood on my own – this was that era now gone, when children still 'played out' on their own. Exactly what my siblings did that afternoon, I'm not sure. All I do know is that, at about 4 p.m., while I was playing with my friend in her driveway, my other sister suddenly appeared, breathless, barefooted (it's strange what you remember).

'You've got to come home', she said. 'Come now. Clare's been run over.'

It's odd how, when something terrible happens, you know straight away that it is terrible. There was no need for my sister to impress on me that this was an emergency. It was obvious by her face, by her eyes, by her voice. I pushed past her; raced up the road. By now my heart was pounding, and my mind was panicking. As I neared the driveway of our house, an ambulance was pulling out. It turned left up the road, away from where I was standing; and as it headed up towards the traffic lights, its siren sounded.

The next few hours, if I'm honest, are a blur. In fact, the next few days are a blur. I have only occasionally delved into those memories, and even at a distance of almost 40 years they are always painful, always raw, and they always throw me slightly off-balance. At some level, I'm sure, I still can't get my head round the fact that our idyllic family life could come to an end in the way it did. That in such a flash our world could change, totally and forever. Even today, the reality of that moment shocks me.

Clare died: but she didn't die straightaway. Perhaps even those few hours prepared us, in some way, for the awfulness of it . . . who knows. All I do know is that a neighbour gave my sister and my brother and me our tea, and looked after us until our tearful, shocked, weary parents eventually returned from the hospital. Clare, they said, was alive – but she was very seriously injured. They would return, first thing in the morning, to find out how she was (back then, in the early '70s, parents weren't encouraged to remain in hospital overnight with their child).

The next morning was terrible. I remember being certain, from the moment I woke up, that Clare was going to die. I have never since felt a dread like those hours. My parents left for the hospital, leaving us with our daily help. The phone kept ringing, and ringing. I remember going upstairs, burying my head in my pillow, wishing it would all turn out to have been a nightmare, failing to comprehend how this could have happened to us.

Eventually, unable, I suppose to cope with the waiting at home, I headed out on my bike. I doubt I was out for more than a few minutes. When I got back, my sister was in the garage. Crying. I remember asking her, 'Is Clare dead?', without really needing to know the answer, because I already knew. My sister wasn't sure, she said, but she had seen our parents coming home, and they were crying. It seemed pretty conclusive: and, indeed, it was.

Over the next few hours – and, in fact, days – my sister and brother and my parents and I stumbled around one another in an almost unbearable, unbelievable sadness. I remember only snatches: finding my mother crying in her bedroom; coming across my father, in tears, phoning the parish priest. Always an immensely courteous, and not very emotional man, he was clearly struggling with the message he had to impart. I remember that he seemed to feel almost guilty at having to infect someone else with the terribleness of what happened to us. 'I'm so sorry to have to tell you, Father, but our youngest daughter died today, in hospital . . . '

What was terrible for my parents, looking back, was having to cope not only with their own searing grief, but having to try to look after the rest of us as well – and with no professional support (there were no children's bereavement services in those days) and, of course, no idea of how best to handle us. What seemed best to them was to make life as normal as possible, and in that, I believe, they were right. But what they didn't realize – and how could they have? – was that we, Clare's sisters and brother, needed to grieve as well. We needed to grieve, as they needed to grieve, on so many levels. And we needed – or at least, I know I certainly needed – some evidence that Clare really was dead. After all, the last time I'd seen her, she'd been playing happily in the back garden. I hadn't seen her injured on the sofa after a neighbour picked her up and carried her to our house. I certainly hadn't seen her lying in a hospital bed, clinging to life.

And after being told she was dead, the lack of hard evidence had continued. I never saw Clare's coffin. I never heard anything about a funeral. My parents – anxious to shield us but failing to comprehend our needs – sent us on an outing, to a zoo, a few days after the accident. I remember, when I returned, realizing with a shock that there had obviously been some kind of event in the house while we'd been out. There were glasses and a stack of plates by the sink. And then I realized, with even more shock, that it must have been the wake after my sister's funeral.

In one sense, things went back to normal very quickly after Clare's death. My father returned to work; the school holiday came to an end; and my sister and brother and I all went back to school. My mother stayed at home, as mothers more often did in the early '70s than they do today. She must have missed her littlest girl so terribly. Clare, after all, had been the child who was around with her during the day – that September, the September after her death, would have been her first term at school.

We started to go back to going on holiday, and to seeing our grandparents, and to visiting friends and doing all the normal things that families do, such as going to the dentist and doing the shopping. Occasionally I'd be aware of someone alluding to Clare's death – I remember the dentist saying to my father that he was 'sorry to hear about your troubles' – but no one ever seemed to come right out and talk about it. Neither inside our family, nor outside it, did Clare seem to merit a mention. Her death had come so quickly, out of nowhere on that sunny afternoon, and now, it seemed, the world had simply moved on and forgotten she ever existed.

I'm not sure whether my parents visited Clare's grave, but they didn't ever take us to see it. I know they felt that we were in the process of moving on, and that to take us there would take us back rather than helping us move on. And then, 7 or 8 months on from her death, came some news that made Clare seem to recede further into our family's memory. My mother was expecting another baby;

and when a little boy arrived, 14 months after her death, we were all carried along on a new wave of excitement and activity. Added to which, just before the baby was actually born, my parents decided that it would be better for all of us if we made a fresh start, and moved away from Manchester where we'd always lived, to the small Pennine town of Mytholmroyd.

Being in a new area seemed to give our family a new start, and make us move on from Clare more quickly than if we'd stayed in the house where she'd spent her life. None of the children at our new school knew that my sister and brother and I had had another sibling; no one in our new parish knew about our still-quite-recent family tragedy. In many ways, I think all this seemed to my parents a good thing, a way of embracing our new future positively. And whereas before we'd been three sisters and a brother, we were now two sisters and two brothers: a family of six once more.

But the problem with unacknowledged grief, as I was later to discover, is that however deeply you bury it, it never, ever goes away. What's more, until you actually confront and deal with it, the grief is always waiting – somewhere inside – to bubble up, and the horrible reality is that undealt-with grief can feel as raw and painful as it did at the very start.

Because I hadn't begun to unpack my grief at Clare's death, I had to bury it very, very deep inside myself. For years and years, I didn't speak about her loss at all – not to anyone. This kind of behaviour certainly isn't my usual modus operandi, so keeping silent about my sister's death was out of character, to put it mildly. What I now recognize is that the grief was simply too terrible to start to sort out. All I could do was to keep it somewhere inside myself, in a box that I was always aware of, but knew I couldn't open. The box was heavy to carry round with me, but I was only too conscious that to open it would be hugely, immensely difficult.

Quite how deeply I buried my grief was brought home to me decades later when, after writing about Clare's death in a national newspaper, I had gone out for dinner with a woman who'd been one of my closest friends at boarding school for 7 years. 'I saw your piece about your sister', she told me. 'I couldn't believe it. You never mentioned her – not in all the years we shared a dormitory.' I couldn't believe it either – had I really kept something that big secret, even from a girl who was at times almost like another sister to me?

The reason I was writing about Clare in a newspaper – not to mention being able to talk about her to my friend – was because, years and years after her death, I did eventually unpack the 'grief box' inside me, and started to deal with what her loss had done to me, and to our family. By the time this happened, I was in my early forties. Decades had passed since Clare's death, and I'd become a journalist, got married, and had four daughters of my own. I'm sure that being a mother made me think more about my youngest sister – in fact, I gave my eldest daughter Clare as her second name – and when each of my daughters was aged between 3 and 4, I was always on super-alert for dangers that might come sweeping out of nowhere, especially on bright, sunny, cloudless days.

So I'm sure it wasn't a coincidence, when my youngest daughter reached the age Clare had been when she died, that I decided I felt strong enough to go back over what had happened, and to try to deal with it in my mind. It was going to be, more than anything, a psychological journey – but I had to make an actual journey, too, to the place where she had been run over, and the place where she was buried.

I hadn't been back to Manchester for some years, but on a chilly March day in 2006 I caught the train from Euston, and headed north. I'd decided to delve into my unexplored grief partly in order to write a feature for my newspaper about the effect of a childhood tragedy. So when I arrived in the city, my first stop was an interview with a children's bereavement counsellor. Within a few minutes of talking to her, I realized that – for possibly the first time in my life – I was with someone who could understand why I was still so upset and confused by my sister's death. And I realized, too, that the counsellor was the first person I'd ever met who understood how the loss of my sister, so long ago, was the key to not just issues in my life, but even to the person I had become.

The counsellor explained to me that, while children can be deeply affected by the death of anyone close to them, it's the death of a parent or sibling that tends to have the most long-term ramifications. If a parent or sibling dies after a long illness, it's an appalling blow, but not as difficult to deal with as a sudden death, like Clare's, when there could be no preparation, no forewarning.

And it's not just the circumstances of what happens when a child is bereaved that determines how well that child deals with the loss. It's what happens afterwards as well. Children who have been bereaved need very sensitive handling if they're going to make it through what's inevitably an incredibly hard experience without lasting psychological scars. They need to be told what's happening; they need to be allowed to ask lots of questions; and if they want, they need to be able to see a coffin or perhaps even the body. They need to see adults grieve, so they can have permission to grieve themselves. They often like to be involved in the funeral – they might like to help choose the clothes in which their relative will be buried or cremated – and they may want to choose keepsakes to put into the coffin.

When the counsellor explained all this to me, it was as though scales fell away from my eyes. Suddenly, I could see why I found Clare's death so difficult to handle, even so many years on – because I'd never really had a chance to grieve her loss. Talking about it now, even at a distance of 34 years, felt as though I was talking about it for the first time . . . which, in a way, I was.

After we'd chatted, I took a taxi to the cemetery where Clare was buried. I'd been there once before, but only many years before. My parents had given me a map to where Clare's grave was, but it took me ages and ages to find it. Just when I'd all but given up hope, there it was in front of me – and how shocking it felt, to be confronted with this, the hard-and-fast evidence that she really was dead, that there really was a grave, and that she really would never, ever be coming back (I'd harboured that dream, for many years).

In the piece I wrote afterwards, I said that being confronted with Clare's grave felt like being punched in the stomach – and I can't improve on that description. Standing there that day, I felt all the sorrow and grief and sadness I might have felt three decades earlier – because, though time is a healer, it only heals if you've done the groundwork. I never had, so this was a starting-point.

Leaving Clare's grave was hard that day, because I felt I was saying goodbye to her for the first time. Over the 4 years since, I've thought about her more than ever – it feels as though I still carry her with me, just as I did before, but now she's lighter and it's not so difficult to have the grief on board. In fact, I've realized that, though Clare had such a short life, and though that life ended so long ago now, she's still alive – in a way – inside me. I feel I've made different choices, and lived a subtly different life, from the one I might have lived if she hadn't died. I feel I'm not as scared of death or being around grieving people as I would perhaps be if I hadn't got a direct experience of death. And I feel that some of the journalistic projects I've got involved with, linked to death, have reflected that.

More importantly, though, I feel I know – at a very deep, visceral level – how precious life is, and how suddenly it can be taken away. In some ways, sometimes, I almost feel as though I owe it to Clare to live every minute and every day as busily and as fully as possible – because she didn't get a chance to live the life I'm living now, with children and a partner and a career and travel and friends and all the things that make adult life interesting and fun.

The other thing I always do is talk about her whenever I can; I talk about her to my daughters, to my siblings, to my friends. It seems like a way of keeping her memory alive, just a little bit. Her life was so short, and she died so long ago, that in many ways it's become entirely irrelevant in the big, busy, wider world. But to me, and my life, she's still hugely relevant – however busy I am, whatever I've got going on, wherever I find myself in the world. And she'll go on being relevant, as long as I'm alive and however old I get. Because in the end, the only thing I can do for Clare is to make sure I never forget her. And that much, I know, I will do.

CHAPTER FIVE

# Paul

Mary Craig

*The writer and broadcaster, Mary Craig, has covered many subjects in print and on the airwaves in a long and distinguished career, including biographies of the Dalai Lama, Lech Walesa, Lord Longford and Pope John Paul II. Blessings, her 1979 account of raising her four children, sold over 250,000 copies worldwide and is regarded by many as a modern spiritual classic. Her severely disabled second son, Paul, died in 1966 aged 10.*

When our 10-year-old son died, most of our friends assumed it was a merciful release. All his life Paul had suffered from a rare and hateful disease – of which there were only a handful of cases in the world. Mentally and physically handicapped, he was hyperactive, doubly incontinent, deaf, mute, and, sadly, had never even recognized my husband, Frank, or myself, let alone had any sort of relationship with us. He was, I must confess, hard to love.

So yes, in many ways it *was* a merciful release. And yet, strangely, that wasn't the whole truth. There had been gain as well as loss – for me, at least. Nothing obvious, perhaps, but the experience of Paul had brought me to a much greater self-knowledge. In the process, I had been dragged out of the wreckage of my old self to become more aware of the sufferings of others. In a very real way Paul had become my teacher. Through him I had embarked on a steep learning curve on which I am still stumbling along. How could I not mourn him?

So I grieved, though I knew in my heart that I was really grieving for the child he might have been. Paul had been difficult from the start, a breech birth during which I lost pints of blood and nearly died, followed by feeding problems – he was insatiable – and screaming day and night virtually non-stop. But we clung to the hope that eventually he would stop screaming and normal life would at last be possible.

I shall never forget the afternoon when we learned the awful truth. It was February 1958 and I had just discovered I was pregnant again. (We had an older son, 3-year-old Anthony.) Paul, almost 2, had been admitted to our local hospital for a hernia operation and for some unexplained reason the house doctor had asked to see me. 'Are you the mother of this child, er, um, Paul Craig?' he began, idly checking the papers on his clipboard. I nodded. 'Well,' he announced in fractured English, 'you know child is not normal. He has gargoylism.' Just like that, off-hand, uncaring. 'Not normal'. 'Gargoylism'!! I had a sickening vision of grotesque stone figures, water gushing out of their drooling mouths. Oh no, no, please, not that.

There was no sympathy on offer, not even a glass of water. Only an indifferent shrug, as he walked out, leaving me to find my own way to the ward where Paul was. How had I not known, I wondered miserably, as I looked at him, my eyes open at last? Oughtn't I to have seen: the stubby fingers, the too-thick lips, the bridge-less nose, the vacant eyes? Well, incredible though it sounds, neither of us had seen those things. We had seen only a pretty baby with big china-blue eyes and glorious curls.

The shock sent my emotions into deep freeze. I turned into a zombie. And when the freeze eventually wore off, it was almost worse. My imagination went into free fall. That horrible word 'gargoylism' was working its poison and I recoiled before a future in which I was some kind of pariah, shunned by everyone. Why, why, why had this happened? Above all, why to *me*, of all people? Abnormality had always filled me with horror. I felt sick at the mere thought of it.

But within a few weeks, I could see that all this rampant self-pity was going to destroy me. Repelled by it suddenly, I realized that I must call a halt. I had reached a crossroads. Either I could go on becoming more and more sorry for myself, losing most of my friends in the process. Or I could come to terms with the fact that, as my situation was not going to alter, it was I who must change. It was a no-brainer, really, a matter of surviving or going under. I had to stop asking, 'why me'? If one thought about it, why *not* me? What was so special about me?

So I tried to face up to things exactly as they were, neither better nor worse, and come to terms with them. It wasn't easy. Accepting the unacceptable never is. It has to be worked at, and the possibility of failure is real. But, I was determined to count my blessings; Frank's never-failing love and support, for one. Many men might have walked away from this situation, but he never complained. Then there were my mother and Aunt Betty who were eager to help. I had Anthony, and by then the new baby, Mark, who seemed to know from day one that he couldn't expect much attention, but thrived on the neglect. The core problem remained – I was still a no-hoper without a life – but from now on I was resolved to put my situation in perspective.

As the days and weeks turned into months and then years, sheer exhaustion began to take its toll. Paul needed constant attention. He was destructive. He couldn't feed himself. He rarely slept. What seemed like a dozen times every night, I would change his nappy and put him back in bed when he was racing round his room laughing like a mad thing; and I remember thinking that it would be like this for ever and ever.

The double incontinence was the worst thing. There were no disposable nappies then and the washing machine – and bath – was in constant use, the house full of disgusting smells. Paul was a force of nature, upsetting Anthony, breaking up his toys, trampling on his precious model ships and aeroplanes, chewing the wheels off his miniature motorcars. What's more, he cheerfully swallowed not only the rubber tyres but every nut, bolt and screw he could lay hands on (they never seemed to do him any harm). He constantly flung the cutlery drawer and its contents to the floor, but when I put it back and shouted at him, he merely chortled and did it again – and again and again. He thought it all a great game.

All this was made worse by the isolation we felt. It is difficult to convey, almost 50 years on, exactly how the mentally handicapped – and their parents – were treated at that time. It was assumed by both the medical profession and some of our friends that a caring and responsible parent would put a child like Paul into an institution and forget about him. (Had they any idea what hell-holes those institutions were?) We were thought irresponsible for keeping him at home. Also, there was no help from social services and none from the community. ('Children like that shouldn't be allowed out', said a woman loudly, when I once of necessity had to take Paul on a bus.) The unspoken thought, both privately and professionally, was that he was a person of no value; and we had no right to imply otherwise.

I recall the endless ghastly trips by ambulance to see medical practitioners, all eager to view this child with the rare and fascinating textbook disease. They praised my 'great contribution to scientific research' (as if I'd had any choice in the matter), while completely blanking me out in their lecture halls as 'the mother' of a freak. As the doctors and their students poked and prodded and

gloated, Paul played to the gallery for all he was worth. I just grit-
ted my teeth and wished I were dead.

When Paul reached school age, we were told to expect a visit
from a doctor who would confirm for the record that he was
ineducable. But the arrival on the front step of a large woman in
tweeds was living proof that, just when you think things can't get
any worse, they do just that. I had barely got the door open before
she gave an excited cluck. 'I can't wait to see this child. Do you think
he might be a cretin?' she asked breathlessly. I could have slammed
the door in her jolly, fat face, but of course I did nothing of the
kind. I was a non-person now, building up a hard shell within
which to protect myself. The only sure way to escape the hurt was
by refusing to acknowledge it. The price of this coping strategy was
that I risked losing my humanity.

The crunch came one day when I was alone in the house with
Paul. I went into his playroom and found that not only had he
soiled himself but was cheerfully smearing the faeces all over himself and the walls. Weeping with frustration, I began to drag him up
the stairs towards the bathroom, ignoring his squawks of protest.
We had got halfway up when the squawks turned into a coughing
fit. Suddenly, he was choking and his face was turning black. I was
panic-stricken, stuck halfway up the stairs with my distressed and
filthy bundle, and nobody within earshot. Summoning the strength
to heave him up the remaining stairs, I shut him in the bathroom
while I raced downstairs to ring for an ambulance, and then rushed
madly up again to run a bath and clean us both up before the
ambulance men arrived with an oxygen cylinder.

That night he almost died, but it turned out to be merely the
first of many bronchial convulsions. I was always being warned to
prepare for his imminent death, but somehow he always came
through. I was torn apart by almost equal measures of love and
resentment. He was my son and I loved him but I had sunk to a

place where I seemed to be trapped in a long dark tunnel from which there was no escape.

Relief was to come in a most unexpected guise. In the summer of 1962, Frank came up with a suggestion: Why not get away for a week? My mother and aunt had just retired from their jobs and would happily take over for a few days. It was a great idea (particularly since my aunt was a nurse), but where on earth could I go? I hated the thought of dragging my own misery around among strangers, or being alone in a hotel room. I had lost the habit of socializing. Then, I had an idea. I could volunteer for work with a charity, if anyone would have me. I was not very experienced, but at least I could cook.

I chose a Home for Concentration Camp Survivors in Cavendish, Suffolk, and they were desperate enough to say yes, please, come ASAP. Cavendish was home to Sue Ryder, who had worked with the Special Operations Executive (SOE) during the war, mainly with young Polish Resistance fighters, and later did post-war relief work in the Displaced Persons camps in Germany. When the international relief agencies eventually packed up in 1949, Sue had stayed on to give personal care to the hard core of homeless and disabled people – mainly Poles – who remained in the camps because nobody wanted them. She was always aware that official charity was not enough, that what these stranded men and women needed was an acknowledgment that they were valued as human beings. When she could find nowhere for them to go, she brought them to her mother's home in Suffolk and cared for them herself.

That visit to Cavendish changed my life forever. I arrived one afternoon, dressed in a good suit and feeling rather noble; but before the end of that first day, having cleaned out a flooded bathroom, peeled countless spuds and helped cook supper for 70, I found myself facing the bitter truth, that I was nothing more than an empty husk with nothing to offer, but plenty to learn.

The survivors swam into my life: Maria, who had lost both her arms when thrown from a moving train by an SS guard, who now did fine embroidery with the needle held in her teeth; white-haired Jozefa, 50 going on 80, a long-term Auschwitz inmate who was one of the few survivors of a final death march; Edward, a Polish lawyer who had suffered in the infamous Pawiak prison in Warsaw before being dispatched to 5 years in the hells of Dachau and Flossenburg; Stefan Bor, who had run an escape-route for Jewish children from the Warsaw Ghetto before being caught by the Gestapo and sent to Auschwitz; and Kazik, a prematurely aged young man, so beaten up by his SS guards that he was a mere vegetable, mute and semi-paralysed. I remember trying to feed him one night, ladling a spoonful of fish into his mouth while tears splashed remorselessly into the spoon.

I had had no idea that such a place existed, that a small Suffolk village was home to survivors of some of the greatest hells ever devised on earth. Here was suffering far beyond anything I could imagine, yet these were remarkable people who seemed to have retained their humanity along with a sense of humour and a child-like wonder. They had been starved, humiliated, tortured, experimented on, stripped of everything and everyone that had given their lives value and meaning, deliberately reduced to the level of sub-humans, scrabbling to stay alive. And yet there was no sign of bitterness. How could I think that, compared with theirs, my own pain was in any way remarkable? I felt ashamed.

At first I was aware only of the horror of so many devastated lives. Then I noticed that I was actually singing as I peeled spuds and onions and beetroots and shared the endless cooking and washing-up. Hard though it was to believe, this was actually a happy place, and I was feeling relaxed for the first time in years. Cavendish was the living proof that it was possible to deal with pain by facing it head on, moving on with it, going beyond it. If men and women could retain their humanity after Auschwitz, then there was hope for us all.

By the end of that week, I already knew the debt I owed these people, but now I had to make sure I did not forget. I came home changed. Frank seemed to understand and offered his support. And my mother and aunt began coming more often, leaving me free in the afternoons to travel all round the north-west of England by bus and train, giving talks, setting up support groups and opening charity shops for what Sue Ryder called her Living Memorial, the prefabricated homes and hospitals she was establishing in Poland, Czechoslovakia and Yugoslavia to care for the sick survivors and their families. The war had been over for 15 years, but the people I spoke to seemed to be as overwhelmed as I had been when learning of the survivors' existence.

Frank and I had not given up hope that something could be done for Paul. (We had already spent time in a Belgian hospital with a doctor who had believed a cure was possible.) Sue Ryder came up with a suggestion. A friend of hers, a Polish neurologist, had, on his release from the horrors of both the Nazi camps and the Soviet gulag, opened a sanatorium for 400 cerebral palsy children in a former barracks outside Warsaw. Sue persuaded him to take Paul into his care and got permission from the Polish Communist authorities for Paul to go to Poland for a 2-year period.

Dr W. came to see us, and we loved him on sight. He didn't treat Paul as an interesting specimen but as a real person, and when he offered an – admittedly slender – hope of improvement, we leapt at the chance. What did we have to lose? Because of his double incontinence, Paul, now 8, had been ejected from his Day Training Centre (a new development within what was still almost non-existent assistance from the state), so he was home all day, face pressed against his playroom window, except when he was hurtling round and round like a maniac. He had been happy at his centre. At least in Poland he would be with other children again.

In the winter of 1963, Paul and I set off for Warsaw. It was without a doubt the best thing we ever did for him. When I left him in Poland a week later, I knew that he was as happy as it was possible for him to be. He actually smiled at me and, though he had no idea who I was, he let me hold his hand. Over the next 2 years I returned several times and could see a distinct change in him, a sort of general contentedness that was new. The bronchial problem had subsided, (the climate obviously suited him). He enjoyed being with the other children and, though they were mystified by him, they seemed fond of him too. He was even learning to feed himself a little, cheerfully helping himself to cake and apples – and his favourites, big green Polish gherkins. When he dropped them on the floor, he just picked them up and crammed them into his mouth.

During these visits, I also travelled all over Poland with Sue in her van laden with provisions, getting to know many more survivors, horrified by the hardships they endured, weeping at their stories, impressed by their stoic cheerfulness and amazing generosity. I made many friends among them.

I was pregnant again. In January 1965 the baby was born – to my horror, with Downs Syndrome, (then called Mongolism), a condition which was completely unrelated to Paul's. We had made medical history; the odds against a combination like that being several hundred thousand to one. When my doctor came in to break the news, he put his head in his hands and wept. As for me, I was near suicidal. It was just so bloody unfair. 'Why me'? raised its ugly head again with a vengeance. When Frank arrived in the afternoon, neither of us could trust ourselves to speak, and we held hands in silence. I absolutely dreaded the night coming on, dreaded the silence, dreaded being left alone with the terror, fury and pain that were raging anew inside me.

Never had the world seemed more bereft of meaning, and never had I been more in need of it. That night I felt myself spiralling downwards into a hell of hopelessness. Then something inexplicable happened: all of a sudden I was no longer falling. Out of the blue some words I had recently glimpsed (idly, no more) in a prayer book that Sue Ryder had given me, flashed into my mind: 'our tragedy is not that we suffer, but that we waste suffering. We waste the opportunity to grow into compassion'. The words flamed out at me, demanding to be looked at, impossible to ignore. It was as though I was being ordered to put my own problems into perspective without delay, to stop feeling sorry for myself and seek instead that compassion, which was nothing less than an openness to the pain of other people's lives.

At the same time I felt myself held in a supportive embrace and a voice inside me said, 'there is a way through this, but you must look for it outside of yourself. Remember you are not alone'. I was mistily aware of a great crowd of camp survivors, and I understood that they were linked by a common thread of suffering and that, now, I too was one with them, linked by that same common thread. I had an overpowering sense of 'all shall be well and all shall be well and all manner of things shall be well'. I have no explanation for any of this, and the experience has never been repeated, but at that moment, I knew that the pain of Nicky's birth would not destroy me. Somehow it would be redemptive, it could be used for good.

Next morning, as the first letters and cards arrived, expressing shock and dismay, I found myself able to reply to them. In some half-understood way, I felt that it was these friends who needed comforting, and I wanted to reach out to them, to pass on to them what I had just learned: that in our darkest, most desolate moments, we may become aware that strength is available for us if we choose to avail ourselves of it. Call it God, call it what you will, it was the most powerful experience I have ever known and I can never forget it.

We called the baby Nicholas Peter and he spent the first months of his life in hospital, strapped to a cot and with tubes sticking out of him every which way. He underwent surgery – he had been born without a rectum, and he too was incontinent. I can't pretend I felt any love for him at first. I rather hoped he'd go away. When he eventually came home from hospital, and in spite of the fact that the washing machine, the smells and the exhaustion once again began to dominate my life, everything was somehow different. Nicky smiled at us, recognized us, was pleased to see us. The whole family fell head over heels in love with him.

It was the start of an enduring love affair, in which he became the heart and centre of all our lives. Choosing to face an uncertain future head on, rather than cling to the train-wreck of past hopes, is perhaps the most important freedom we possess. As Viktor Frankl affirmed in his wonderful *Man's Search for Meaning*, 'everything can be taken from a man but one thing: the last of the human freedoms – to choose one's attitude in any given set of circumstances, to choose one's own way'.

We knew now that Paul was not going to get better. The bronchial pneumonia had returned, and Dr W. could do no more. Nevertheless the telegram from Poland came as a huge shock, arriving as it did on a bitterly cold December afternoon at the end of that year, 1965. 'Child desperately ill. Come at once.'

The Polish Embassy in London arranged for me to collect a visa the next morning. By nightfall, I was in East Berlin, where our

Warsaw-bound plane was grounded for a full 24 hours due to fog and ice. It was 2 days after the telegram had arrived when I reached the sanatorium where Paul lay fighting for his life, breathing heavily, a cylinder of oxygen by his bed. The shadow of death lay over him.

It was freezing cold in Warsaw. For the next 2 days, I scurried between the Polish Ministry of Health, the British Embassy, and the Lot Airlines office, making arrangements for our journey back to England. Within a week all the preparations were in place. The return journey, as anyone could have predicted, was a nightmare, though everyone concerned tried to make things as easy as possible. The ambulance which brought us from the sanatorium was allowed right up to the plane steps, and as the plane was only half-full we had a whole row of seats to ourselves, complete with oxygen cylinder. At Heathrow, where we were in transit, we were escorted to a private room where a nurse was waiting. And when we reached our home airport, Ringway, in Manchester, Frank was able to drive his car up to the plane.

So next morning, there they both were, Paul and Nicky under the same roof for the first time, neither of them aware of the other's existence. Paul was now a heavy nursing case, condemned to spend what remained of his life in a bed, unable to move without help. How on earth were we going to manage?

Joe, our GP, was in no doubt. 'You can't keep him at home', he said firmly. 'It wouldn't be fair to any of you'. He mentioned a hospital about 20 miles away, and began to make arrangements to transfer Paul there. Then I panicked. I couldn't just send Paul to die among strangers. There had to be another way. But were any of us physically strong enough to look after him at home? Betty and I came to an agreement. She would help cope with Paul through the week, if I would take over at weekends. Joe was horrified – he didn't believe we could possibly manage for even 24 hours – but he agreed we should give it a try.

So Betty stayed for the rest of that difficult week, and on Friday Frank and I nervously took over. Somehow we got through the weekend, though it was a tough call. Paul was suffering. Whenever I turned him over onto his side, sat him upright, dressed or undressed him, washed him, changed his pants, he whimpered miserably. Sores were multiplying; his body had become an intolerable burden to him. There was nothing for him to do, no solace for him anywhere.

But we had survived the weekend, and I felt almost euphoric. Next time it would be easier, I assured Betty, when she returned on the Sunday evening.

There was no next time. The following Friday morning, 10 February 1966, Betty found Paul dead on the floor by the side of his bed. He had fallen out of bed and suffered a heart attack, dying alone and frightened, in the dark, while we slept.

Writing this now has brought with it a lot of pain, but also some surprising insights. It has suddenly hit me that those parents who have experienced a stillbirth – or a baby who dies within a few days of birth – must have the same sense of being cheated by life. Paul was with us for 10 years, but I knew him no better at the end of that time than at the beginning. He was unknowable. Ask me about him and I can tell you that as a baby he had blue eyes and blonde curls. Beyond that – nothing. He was with us, yet not with us.

Afterwards, of course, there was guilt amid the sadness. Yet what hurt most in the days that followed his death was the general assumption (not within the family, I have to say) that Paul's life had been a useless irrelevance, a disaster best forgotten. Even in the middle of sometimes extremely conflicting emotions, I was convinced that it was not really so. If our value as human beings lies in what we do for each other, Paul's gift to me had been immense. He had challenged me to face up to my situation, and had led me to discover reserves buried so deep that I hadn't even known they existed. 'It is only with the heart that one can see rightly. What is essential is invisible to the eye', as the Little Prince's fox so wisely told him.

Paul lived on in Nicky, but this time it was all so different. Nicky knew and loved us, laughed and played with us. Although he was incontinent until he was 16 (when he had a colostomy), we learned from a consultant when he was just 2 that there was no reason why he would not be able to speak, and that gave us hope. And when he actually did begin to speak (in however garbled a fashion), it was a major miracle. We set our sights low. If we expected nothing, there was no chance of being disappointed, and the least sign of progress could be a source of wonder.

As the years passed, there were many such signs. Nicky was a life-enhancer. A friend of ours wrote about him in the Catholic journal *The Tablet*: 'Nicky will never build a car, or fly an aeroplane, or balance a set of accounts. But he never stops producing joy and love wherever he goes. He is a year-round Christmas gift, however crumpled his wrapping'.

Today, more than 45 years later, Nicky (now Nick) is still at home. Frank died many years ago, but Anthony has come to live with me, and Mark and his family are nearby. We often quote that last sentence to Nick when he's sulking or being stroppy. In spite of his age and his many abilities, he remains a child in many ways and still needs us, but there's no denying that he's an invaluable member of our family and an extraordinary source of joy – a year-round Christmas gift indeed.

Long ago, I wrote a book about my experiences and called it *Blessings*. Its main purpose was to suggest that it is not the external happenings of our lives that shape us, but how we choose to respond to them. We have to continue to act like human beings within our altered circumstances, and try to turn the experience to good. I was not enamoured of the title, and tried many times before publication to change it, but my publishers insisted on it. When the letters began pouring in, I realized that they were right. My life had been rich in blessings, and the biggest blessing of all was – and is – Nick. And it was Paul who helped me to understand.

# CHAPTER SIX

# *Charles*

## Louise Patten

*Louise Patten is a novelist and businesswoman. She was one of the first women to chair a FTSE company, is Senior Advisor to Bain & Company, and is currently a director of Marks and Spencer and of UKAR. She published her first novel,* Bad Money, *in 2009, and followed it with* Good As Gold *in 2010. Her brother, Charles, died in 1962 aged 10.*

Water was the constant of our childhood. A narrow-tracked quagmire of unreclaimed salt marsh led from the bottom of our garden right down to the north-Essex mudlands, a glorious desolation of rotting breakwaters, stilt-legged birds and seaweed-pods that exploded into stinking, watery jelly. After school, a pleasant sanctuary of nuns and encouragement, and once we'd eaten the peanut-butter sandwiches that were a compulsory source of energy in those days, the afternoons were free. There were crabs in the mud for bare-toed dares, sluice gates to slither over, and the threat of dozing adders in the dunes beyond the backwaters. Most exciting of all, once we'd crossed the inlet of sucking ooze at its base, there was the drowning ash tree to climb. I never got further than quavering on the lowest branch, with my sister dangling high above me and my brother doing brave things 100 feet up.

With Frinton only 2 miles away, the sea was a clean alternative to the brackish waters of the Naze. Beach-hut afternoons involved the inevitable peanut-butter sandwiches supplemented with shrimps caught in the shallows and boiled up over the primus stove, but once we were judged to have absorbed enough protein, we could do what we liked. Swimming during thunderstorms was the best, when the whole wide sea was ours alone and we could frighten ourselves with the threat of lightning electrocutions. When the sun shone, there were sand-jumps to build, starfish to rescue from dehydration, and the hideously globular transparency of jellyfish to chop with our spades.

When we weren't beside the sea, we were on it. *Sundowner* had been our grandfather's boat, a 60-foot motor-yacht into which he'd famously crammed over 100 British soldiers, dodging German planes to bring them all safely home from the beaches of Dunkirk. We were proud of the Little Ships' pennant in *Sundowner*'s flag-locker, and proud too of our own handiness on deck. In reality, my timidity doubtless kept me clinging to the guard-rails, though memory sees me alongside Anne-Marie and Charles, crewing the boat across the Channel and scaling the sides of the cavernous locks of central France.

If there were clouds in the skies of our 1950s childhood, they seemed to be small ones. Charles tried to balance on a beach ball and broke his arm. Anne-Marie was stung by a Portuguese man-of-war and had to go to hospital. There was a dead sister, too, our parents' first child. But she'd died the month before Anne-Marie was born so none of us had known her and her name was rarely mentioned. Apart from my personal interest in her emerald brooch, a christening present which had unaccountably been passed on to me, 'God bless Katherine,' seemed just a parroted footnote to our night-time prayers.

Then quite suddenly, a shadow crept over the rim of our horizon as school conversations began drifting out from the drawing room. It was never explained, but we gathered that while the local convent could teach Anne-Marie and me all that it was necessary for girls to learn, Charles' education involved a completely different concept. He had to go to a proper Catholic prep school, and this meant leaving home, the sea, the backwaters and moving to London to share our grandmother's house.

For sea-bred children, Richmond Slipways could have been a great deal worse. It was beside the Thames, pitifully narrow, constrained by concrete, but water nevertheless. There was a stub-sterned pram dinghy in which we learned to row, and *Sundowner* was moored at the foot of the garden, always available for trips across the Channel, or for when we just wanted to sleep in a bunk. But for my 7-year-old self, the switch from rural Essex to city life was too abrupt. I hated London, though Charles did what he could to help. Every week, he gave me his pocket money and quite a few of his other small treasures as well. He took me to the swings at the Old Deer Park because I was too young to go on my own. He'd even hold my hand in the street, a considerable sacrifice for a 10-year-old boy.

Perhaps our parents noticed how miserable I was, because one afternoon we were taken to the circus on Richmond Green. I loved the spangled ponies, and the clowns made Charles laugh so much that he was sick all over our feet. Not long afterwards, he started being sick even when he wasn't laughing, so he was taken away somewhere for tests. He was gone for several nights, and when he came home again, a blanket of silence fell, inhibiting us from asking many questions. He was ill; he would get better; that was all. We just had to expand our standard daily prayers to include special petitions for his recovery.

When I was invited to write this essay, I rang my sister to see what she thought about my doing it. Anne-Marie and I are very close, but the odd thing was that I had no idea how she'd feel. We'd simply never spoken about Charles since he first became ill. After some debate she and I agreed that this was something we should talk about, though it wasn't an easy decision. Our silence had been so complete that it felt somehow irreverent to break it and to exhume distress that had been buried for decades .

For Anne-Marie, five years older and more perceptive than I, her overwhelming memory was of the state of Panglossian denial our family slipped into. Everything was for the best. Naturally Charles would recover. The reality of his cancer was nullified. Even the full-length mirror in the hall was taken down so that Charles shouldn't see how emaciated he'd become – and if he couldn't see it, then neither should we. Used to trusting our parents and with nothing else to go on, Anne-Marie had believed the pretence that Charles wasn't particularly ill, and would recover in due course. This lack of any preparation for the truth meant that she was entirely blind-sided when one of her friends passed on an overheard comment that he was dying. After that, or perhaps after the tearful questions that must have followed, my sister was packed off elsewhere for the duration.

For my part, having younger and less well-informed friends, I never doubted that Charles would get better, despite the horrors of his illness. The pain made him scream a lot; high, thin screams that went on for hours. I knew I could help if our parents would let me. Those terrible cries pulled me to his room again and again. Each time I'd peer round the door, only to be told to go away. I was too noisy, Charles needed absolute calm, he couldn't bear to have me near him. I didn't believe them. Of course he wanted me there, my brother loved me and I loved him. But I'd creep off anyway, afraid of the helpless, blank-eyed looks I'd get from my mother and father.

When Charles wasn't screaming, there'd be a nervous interval of silence. I soon learned to slip down to my grandmother's end of the house, where we'd watch her black and white television or talk about my late grandfather, Commander Lightoller, heroic survivor of *Titanic* as well as of Dunkirk. My grandmother managed the situation by keeping me chatting about her husband's extraordinary life and the truth behind the *Titanic* mythology, perhaps trying to disguise the fact that my brother's merciful periods of quiet had spread, rather less mercifully, to my parents. But being lame and semi-housebound, she couldn't take me out, which would have been the only effective way to prevent me from looking and fretting.

Children observe their families closely, though they may not dare to ask questions. I watched as my mother and father first stopped touching each other, then stopped smiling, and eventually seemed to stop talking altogether. After a while, those helpless sessions absorbing their son's pain became solitary vigils, as if they couldn't bear being in the same room together. Even the ritual of one of them coming up to say my night prayers with me ceased, though that didn't stop my confident pleas to God, Our Lady, and every saint whose name and special powers I could remember, to make my brother well again soon.

One day, with no explanation and the minimum amount of fuss, Charles vanished to Guy's Hospital. Anne-Marie and I weren't allowed to visit our brother there, and we never saw him again. There were still occasional bulletins: he was comfortable, he'd never be in pain again, perhaps he'd be home soon. Without the constant reminder of his screams, I became optimistic, planning treats and surprises for when he was well enough to share them.

On a Sunday afternoon when both Anne-Marie and I happened to be at home, our parents turned up. It was unusual in that they were normally at the hospital till late, and even more so that they had come back together – though this only lasted for the time it took them to walk down the still-unmirrored hall, after which my sister and I were taken off to separate rooms.

I was led into the kitchen by our mother. She shut the door behind her, took one of my hands and said, 'Charles doesn't need us any more.' I was overjoyed. If he didn't need them at the hospital, he must truly be getting better.

'That's wonderful! When's he coming home?'

'He isn't coming home to us. He's gone to be with God.'

My sister, meanwhile, had been taken into the drawing-room by our father. Half a lifetime later, when I finally asked Anne-Marie about it, she still remembered his exact words: 'Charlie's gone to heaven.'

She also remembers her shocked reply, 'Oh, has he?' and her immediate distress that she hadn't come up with something more comforting to say.

Anne-Marie is certain that she didn't cry, and I can't remember crying then either, nobody did. Whether it was the reticence of those post-war years or because it was simply too painful to articulate, the word 'death' was never used, and for me that made the whole thing impossible to believe. Surely my parents had made a mistake? Charles was still alive. He'd be home soon, in time for Christmas, certainly.

As if our family earthquake had never happened, we were sent to school the next day as normal. My form teacher put an arm round me and said how sorry she was. When she started weeping, I began to think that Charles really might be dead, after all. I'd never dreamed that nuns *could* cry. Meanwhile in the senior part of the school, my sister remembers the announcement of our brother's death at morning assembly. The shock of something so private becoming public made it real, and then she too cried.

There were no tears on the day of Charles' funeral, or at least none was shed in front of us. There was just the stiff tableau of our parents, worryingly dressed in unbroken black, standing silent and apart while my grandmother – blessedly still wearing her normal dove grey and lilac – gave them small glasses of sherry. Anne-Marie and I were excluded from our brother's funeral, just as we had been from his illness and death. I'd have liked to be able to visit his grave but I've no idea where he's buried; at the time, the question would have been impossible to ask either of my parents, and it's too late now as both are dead.

In the following months, our grief was buttoned in by a polite silence while our family unit disintegrated into its individual component parts. Anne-Marie was posted off to boarding school 100 miles away, as if it was some kind of punishment. It was never explained that the money set aside for Charles' education was being used instead to give her an academic leg-up. The next severance was when our father went off on his own, taking the large houndstooth check suitcase with him. I remember trailing after him along the river-bank, imploring him not to go, in what was presumably a painful scene for my father. At the time, he assured me that he'd be back soon, but it was a lie. I subsequently found out that our parents were divorcing and he'd never be home again.

To say that this was a gloomy period would be otiose, but there were consolations. I spent increasing amounts of time with my grandmother, developing a wonderfully close relationship that lasted until her death, many years later. At school, too, the Sisters of Mercy came into their own, providing comfort with a complete absence of mawkishness. It was quite right to grieve, they explained – but not in excess. I should always remember that Charles was in heaven and he wouldn't want to look down and see me miserable, would he? When I questioned God's existence, they answered as rationally as if I were an adult. Faith was a one-way bet. Belief in heaven helped you to be good, which in turn helped you to happiness in the afterlife. If it turned out that no such afterlife existed, you'd lost nothing, whereas if you lived a bad life and subsequently found that heaven did indeed exist, you'd have eternity to regret your mistake.

Many decades have passed, but Pascal's Wager still makes sense to me and stoked some useful sisterly debate when Anne-Marie and I needed a break from digging up our memories of Charles' death. Ultimately, we found that we could look back in pity at the double loss our parents had suffered. Silence and a stiff upper lip must have been the only way they felt they could cope with the loss of their only son, yet we can also see how our parents could have managed things better – had we only dared to tell them.

The first thing we might have said would have been that a dead child can never be replaced, though in 1948 when our elder sister was born, accepted medical opinion was the exact opposite. Katherine was a beautiful baby, golden haired and violet eyed, but she had a heart defect which in those days was inoperable. When our parents were given the news that Katherine wasn't going to survive beyond her first birthday, they were advised to have another baby immediately, as if a second child could compensate for the loss of their first. As a result, Anne-Marie was born a scant month after Katherine's death, too soon to allow a quiet period for grief, too robustly healthy to allow any sort of bonding with a mother who'd spent the past year nursing an invalid baby.

Our parents' marriage must have been strong to have survived the loss of their first child, and in many ways they were well matched. Both practising Catholics, our father was a quietly witty, jazz-loving classicist. Our mother was the more outgoing of the two, also musical and a passionate linguist. During the sea-side years, they walked, talked and gardened together, laughing over the foibles of Frinton, enjoying the summer theatre, and agonising over preparations for the absurdly formal dinner parties of the 1950s. If they hadn't allowed themselves to stop talking, a solid marriage could even have been strengthened by them sharing their grief when Charles died.

But then the loss of two children might wreck all but the strongest of marriages. Charles was the only boy, and a particularly enchanting child as well, so perhaps our parents' sorrow was just too deep to share with anyone, even each other. In subsequent years, my mother rarely talked about her dead children, and then only briefly and in response to some direct question. My father never referred to them at all. For my part, I've thought about Charles every single day since he died, but from my father's complete silence, I'd always assumed he'd somehow managed to shut away all memory of his son. I found out too late that I'd been wrong. My father's fatal heart attack was on 18 April, Charles' birthday. He'd been walking to Mass. It turned out that he went to Mass on Charles' birthday always – I wish I'd known.

There was so much that Anne-Marie and I didn't know, and second only to our parents' divorce, their inability to explain the truth to us was the hardest thing to cope with. Although we were young, we saw and heard far more than our parents presumably thought children did. In our own separated worlds, Anne-Marie and I both worried desperately about our parents, but thinking it was the right thing to do, we copied them and kept our anxieties to ourselves. Neither of us knew how to behave in those extreme circumstances, so perhaps our self-control made us seem unfeeling?

Whatever the reasons, our parents' reticence made things worse for us. It would have been much less frightening to have seen our parents crying together instead of their dreadful, silent apart-ness.

Mourning together as a family would have helped, too, and if we'd been allowed to go to Charles' funeral, I might have accepted that he was really gone instead of spending the rest of my childhood half-believing he'd come back.

The period after his death might have been improved if we'd been encouraged to exchange memories of our dead brother. Although his death meant that our family life was inevitably going to be changed forever, remembering all the happy years we'd spent with Charles would have helped us to absorb the loss and make it into a positive thing, because like misery, happiness is infectious. The 18th of April was always a day to dread, a date to tiptoe around, to hold one's breath in case it slipped out by mistake. How much better might it have been if we'd been open about what we were all thinking? If we'd bought each other presents and had actually celebrated Charles' birthday?

Photographs would have helped us to hold onto happy memories, too. After Anne-Marie and I had talked ourselves out, we searched for all the old photos of our childhood which had been shut away since Charles' death. And suddenly there we were again, the three of us, playing on Frinton beach, splashing through the backwaters, swimming off *Sundowner*, even in our usual positions up the ash tree – and in every single picture, we're all grinning.

Those old images were proof that we'd been happy before Charles' death, and so we have been since. The period of his illness was cruel, the unhappiness after was worse, but life went on and the pain got better. Even at the time, good came out of bad. For Anne-Marie, the boarding school she was sent away to was St Mary's, Shaftesbury, and it provided the alternative family she needed. She arrived as 'the girl whose brother just died,' to find near-instant friendships and a support network which has lasted to this day.

## Charles

My schooling followed a different route. I determined to replace my parents' lost son, intellectually at least, by becoming a quasi-boy. Hoping to please my father by going to his old university, I went to Oxford when fewer than 10 per cent of undergraduates were female. I subsequently followed his footsteps into the City in pursuit of what was then a 'male' career. Unfortunately, rather than delighting my father, I realized too late that this breach of his conventions had really distressed him. My mother, on the other hand was surprisingly proud, and the path I chose – one I'd never have taken but for my brother's death – has been a satisfying one for me.

Both Anne-Marie and I have children, and as parents ourselves, the death of a child is unimaginable. The death of a sibling was miserable, but whether well-handled or not, the pain does recede. I'll never forget Charles, not even for a day. His rosary is by my bed. He was holding it when he died, and I now hold it every night, feeling my brother's presence, benign and joyful, just as he was on earth.

# CHAPTER SEVEN

# *Tracy*
## Kim Meade

*Kim Meade is a mother and grandmother who lives alone in west London. Her older daughter, Tracy, went missing in 1992 at the age of 14. Her body was found, 2 weeks later, in a local canal.*

It was a very cold January that year. My sister, Jackie, and a couple of female friends had come round to my flat for the evening. It was Monday 20 January 1992. We were having chilli con carne and I put on some music. Then Tracy asked if she could go round to see her cousin, Kelly, my sister's daughter, who was her age. She often went there, so we agreed. It was only a 10-minute walk, and it wasn't late – 7 o'clock in the evening. She'd stay the night and head off straight to school the next morning.

I had no real reason to worry. Tracy was coming up 15 that March but had never given me any cause for concern. If we had a row, she might slam the door, but the next minute she'd be back, giving me a kiss and saying she was sorry. She had lots of friends, a big gang of girls, and they did all the things that teenage girls like to do – hair, make-up, clothes. They went back and forth from each other's houses, but my rule was that she always had to be in by 9 p.m. There was no night-clubbing or anything like that.

We didn't have a lot, but we were happy. Our flat was on the sixth floor of a tower block on the Warwick Estate in west London. Tracy's dad wasn't living with us anymore, but he was in touch. At home there was just me, Tracy and her sister, Tanya, who was 9 years younger. My mum was nearby and Tracy was close to her. She'd sometimes sleep over there to keep her company. Tracy was doing alright at school and was planning to study child care, but I had been having a bit of trouble with the local authority over getting her a bus pass to help pay for her fares so she'd missed a few days.

She said goodbye and went to her cousin's. I remember how she looked. She had her brown hair up. When she was little, people said she looked just like her father, whose family are Greek, but as she had grown up, she became more like me. She wasn't very tall, but she was slim and had green-blue eyes.

The first alarm bell rang the next day when I got a call from my mum saying Tracy had never arrived at my sister's. I just didn't know what to think, but I tried not to panic. I told myself there must be an explanation. There were no mobiles back then. Today, I'd be able to ring at once and find out where she was, but all I could do was begin contacting her other school friends to see if she'd stopped over with one of them. She'd never done that before without asking, but they were teenagers after all.

No one had seen her. They were all together 7 days a week but suddenly it was as if she'd vanished. I started looking anywhere I could think she might have gone. My sister-in-law, Anne-Marie, was helping me, but there was no sign of Tracy. So on the Wednesday I went to the police station on the Harrow Road.

I didn't get beyond the front desk. They took my details and Tracy's, but they said she had probably stayed out with her friends, and now was frightened to come home in case I told her off. That didn't feel right to me. She had never done anything like that before and had no reason to go off. She wasn't talking to her dad at the time, because he had been cross when he caught her smoking, but apart from that, there was nothing. She had never been grounded. She had never been hit. I tried to explain that to the police, but they weren't offering to do anything more at that stage. It was down to us.

I couldn't sleep so Anne-Marie and I and other members of my family were going in and out of the local shops, anywhere we thought she might have been, showing them photos, asking them questions, in case anyone remembered anything. Someone said they thought they had seen Tracy down at Shepherd's Bush, so we went there, hoping someone would give us some clue as to where she was.

Eventually one of her friends told me that there was an older boy, who liked her, who lived on Edgeware Road. I rang the doorbell, but the boy wouldn't let me in. He just opened the door a crack and said he hadn't seen her. I wasn't satisfied. I had a feeling she was in the house, so I went back to the police on Thursday. This time I saw someone in CID. They got a warrant and sent two officers with me to search the house. It was a mess, but there was no sign of her there.

In our flat I went through her things, looking for clues. I couldn't find any. Her jewellery was still there. Her chain was there, hanging up, and at my mum's we found her rings. She hadn't taken anything. It was as if she'd disappeared into thin air.

It had been my boyfriend's birthday a few days before Tracy went missing and he'd got a watch for his present. He'd let Tracy borrow it and that had gone missing with her, so Anne-Marie suggested we check the local pawnbrokers in case someone had tried to get money on it, but again there was no sign. In one place, I remember they even asked Anne-Marie and me if we were policewomen.

There was too much going on in my head at the time to wonder why the police weren't helping us more. Two of my brothers had been in trouble with the law over glue-sniffing so our family was known to them. I can only think they had us down as some kind of problem family and thought that Tracy was a runaway. Or that someone in the family knew what had happened to her. I felt judged. Tracy's disappearance wasn't a priority.

I tried to contact the newspapers, and rang the *Sun*, but they told me I had to go through a lawyer. I was lost. I didn't know which way to turn, who I could ask to help me. And all the time my daughter had been missing for longer and longer.

Tanya was staying with my brother and his wife. If I fell asleep during those days, it would only be for an hour and then I'd wake up, and as I woke up I wanted it so badly to be a dream, for Tracy to be there. That feeling still happens to me some days first thing in the morning. I hope it is a dream and then the nightmare is back.

You didn't hear so much about children being snatched then, and so I tried not to think the worst, tried to convince myself that she'd gone to one of her friends, and that she was frightened of showing her face now that there had been such a fuss about her going missing. I just felt so struck. I didn't know what to do, what more to do. So we just carried on searching as the days went by. The police dropped in every day, sometimes twice, to see if she'd come home, or ask if I'd found anything out.

Suddenly it was Sunday and Tracy had been gone for almost 2 weeks. I was at my flat in the evening, getting things ready to go out looking again the next morning, when two policemen came round. A young boy had been fishing in the Regent's Canal, up by Kensal Rise Cemetery, not that far from my flat, and his hook had caught on the back a T-shirt. He had pulled a body out. That had been the previous day. They thought it might be Tracy. They asked me again what she had been wearing. When I told them, they said that it sounded like it might be Tracy, but told me I would have to wait until the next day because the mortuary was closed.

I didn't sleep a wink that night. My dad and Tracy's dad went the next day to see the body. When they told me it was her, I shut myself in the front room and couldn't stop crying. It took a while for the details to sink in. The police said she was clean and had eaten, but they were unclear whether she had been in the canal all two weeks, or had been somewhere else first. She hadn't been sexually assaulted. That was one small mercy. But she had been stabbed. What had killed her, though, was drowning. She was a strong swimmer. I think she was must have been trying to get away from them, whoever they were, but the water was so cold.

After we identified her body, the police launched a murder enquiry. There was even an appeal on *Crimewatch*. The papers suddenly got interested, but not always in a good way. One tabloid suggested Tracy was a glue-sniffer, like my brothers, but I know that wasn't true. I know the signs. I would have spotted it.

They pulled in all sorts of people for questioning, but no one was ever charged. The file is still open to this day. So I don't know what happened to Tracy between when I saw her last and her death in that cold canal. There was ice on the water. Not knowing tortures me. Someone, somewhere out there does know, but I am her mother and I have no idea. I could be saying hello to the person who murdered Tracy when I'm walking down the road. It must have been someone she knew. Tracy wouldn't have gone off with a stranger. And the watch has never been found, but on her fingers were rings I had never seen. I go over and over it in my head.

We finally were allowed to bury Tracy in the April. After that the whole police enquiry went quiet. It was my family who supported me through it, and still do. There have been times, if I am honest, when I thought about ending it, but I had Tanya and I lacked the courage. A few months after Tracy died, I stated to suffer from agoraphobia. I was just walking down the street when this terrible fear came over me. I didn't know which way to go, whether to go forwards or backwards. It is still with me.

In a strange way, I am thankful that they did find her body, that she didn't remain another name on a list of missing people. I didn't see her after they found her. I preferred to remember her as she was. I have a pendant round my neck always with a picture of her taken shortly before she disappeared. She is smiling.

I moved soon afterwards. I didn't go far, but I couldn't stay in that flat. I have kept all Tracy's things. Her clothes are all neatly packed away. I have her record player. Sometimes I go back in my mind to the day she was born. It was Mother's Day and I remember that at first, she didn't cry. I'd thought I'd lost her then.

I have her photographs always around me. I kiss her every morning and talk to her. And I talk about her to people. I don't want people to think they can't mention her. I don't go out much now. I've tried counselling and that helped a bit. I used to go to meetings of other parents who had been in similar circumstances. They were good, but I don't like travelling anywhere. I get panic attacks.

For a long time I didn't even have a phone. Now I enjoy my grandchildren, Tanya's children, when they come over, but otherwise all the happiness seems to have drained out of life. I sit at home on my own. I don't bother with papers and the news.

I feel as if Tracy is here with me, every day and every night. But so is the mystery of what happened to her. Perhaps if I could find out what happened to her, my life wouldn't feel as if it's on hold.

# CHAPTER EIGHT

# *Archie*

## Robin Baird-Smith

*Robin Baird-Smith is a writer and distinguished publisher who has held senior posts at HarperCollins, Constable and Duckworth. He is currently publishing director at Continuum. His son, Archie, was killed in a car crash in 1994 at the age of 14.*

> 'Je n'enseigne point. Je raconte', Michel de Montaigne

The facts are simply told. What happened, happened in a split second.

On 8 January 1994, my wife and I and our middle child, Archie, were driving back from Dorset. We had been thinking of buying a small cottage and had joined the A303 road just north of Shaftesbury. It was late afternoon and very dark.

At 4.50pm, a young man in a white Volvo car drove into us at 70 miles an hour. I can remember the impact clearly. By an error of judgement, imagining it to be a dual carriageway, he was driving up the wrong side of the road. I was unconscious for 50 minutes. How I survived I do not know.

When I came round, I felt very cold but I did manage to reel off a whole lot of telephone numbers so my relatives could be informed. My wife, Sarah, was sitting beside me, secured by her safety belt.

She looked beautiful, radiant. I did not know she was dead. My son, Archie, about whom I most want to write in these pages, was fatally injured on the back seat and unconscious.

He lived for 2 days. He was taken to Southampton Hospital Neurological Unit but his case was hopeless. I never saw him again.

I was taken by ambulance to Salisbury General Hospital. Just as I was wheeled into the operating theatre for orthopaedic surgery, the surgeon told me that my wife was dead. I thanked him for being so professional and for telling me immediately.

The novelist William Trevor once wrote: 'I know that losing a child is different from losing a wife. You have lost your wife and your past. With the death of the young it is the future.'

Ultimately, the death of Archie has been the greater pain, the greater sadness for me. He was 14. But nature has its way of helping us to cope with such sadness. It is called shock. If one realized fully at the time how terrible such losses are, one might not survive them. So for shock, one must be profoundly grateful. It is a kind of numbing of the senses.

In *A Grief Observed*, C. S. Lewis describes the sensation as a feeling of being mildly drunk, concussed. There is a kind of invisible blanket between oneself and the world. Because of the shock, I was unnaturally cheerful in those early days. People who came to visit me in hospital, expecting to find me in a heap, were amazed to find me making jokes. This was not courage. It was not optimism. It was shock.

Above all I seemed to be completely devoid of anger. Early on, I became very resentful and irritable on the subject of religion. A nurse in the hospital, no doubt with the best intentions, told me to 'turn my mind to the Man Upstairs'. This enraged me.

I also became deeply anti-clerical. I am a Roman Catholic, but the presence of priests became quite irksome to me. I realized later that this was a kind of sublimated anger against God. The only priest who did not irk me was a young Dominican who visited me in hospital and simply said, 'I don't know what to say'. That made two of us.

But let me go back. In a strange way, I think the soul, the psyche, has a sense in advance of big events in people's lives. Certainly of death. When I was 18, my mother gave me a book for a present by Laurence Whistler called *The Initials in the Heart*. Laurence was the brother of the celebrated artist Rex Whistler. He was himself a considerable poet and a glass engraver of genius. He had married a beautiful actress called Jill Furze who had died 4 years later of cancer. The book is his poetic account of their life together. It is entirely unsentimental. I was struck by something he wrote and copied it down in my notebook. 'The more one suffers, the more one's capacity for gaiety increases'. I shall come back to this, and to Whistler, later on.

When Sarah and I became engaged in 1975, we went to the opera together to see Gluck's *Orpheus and Eurydice* at Covent Garden. As the orchestra played the celebrated 'Dance of the Blessed Spirits', she tapped me on the arm and said to me: 'That is the music I want at my funeral'. And so it was to be.

In September, before the car accident, we all went to the Crimea for a family holiday. I took with me to read the collection of short stories by Chekhov called *Lady with Lapdog*. In this collection there is a story simply called 'Grief'. In it a farmer drives his wife to hospital in a carriage because she is critically ill. After a while, he can hear her body, her bones, thudding against the side of the carriage behind him. He knows she is dead. This story gripped me. I could feel that thudding resonating and reverberating in my own bones. I still re-read the story from time to time.

The night before our accident, Sarah and I went to see a performance of *An Inspector Calls* by J. B. Priestley. On stage was a huge iron edifice, a structure which is a house. At a certain point, with a terrible crash, the edifice collapses with so many hopes and illusions with it.

*   *   *

First, let me tell you a bit about Archie. He was, as I have said, 14 at the time of his death. He had been at St Paul's School in Barnes, London, for only one term. Archie was an essential bridge between his elder brother, Max, and his younger sister, Leonora. With Max he shared a passion for sport – cricket and football. Sarah had erected nets in our back garden. They used to play many evenings in the summer.

Recently, I found one of Archie's school exercise books. It contained a short essay called 'My Hobbies'. In it he wrote: 'My most joyful hobby is playing football with my brother – except we usually end up fighting'.

With Leonora he shared pranks and jokes. They were always, as I remember, laughing, singing songs, giggling.

Sam was Archie's best friend. They were brought together by a desire to be extremely naughty. I keep in touch with Sam. This is important to me. He is now married and enjoying early success as a television director and writer. Sam wrote recently: 'I cannot think of Archie as a child, but as someone older than me. It's probably because all my friends and I always looked up to him so. He was always the cleverest, the best sportsman and the one with the wittiest insults!'

Archie was a natural linguist and showed early signs of being a fine musician. We did not need to nag him to practise the violin. He just did it of his own volition. In just one term at his new school, he had made significant progress in learning Italian and had played second violin in a stirring end of term performance of Walton's 'Crown Imperial March'.

He showed an early interest in the opposite sex. He could be extremely charming.

Archie was very fast on his feet. Any of my attempts to wallop him were fruitless, as he moved so much faster than me.

* * *

As soon as I returned to London and got back into a routine – bringing up my two remaining children, slowly getting back to work – I was advised to embark on a compensation claim. Not that it would bring Sarah and Archie back to us, but it would be a concrete way in which we could express our anger at what had happened to us.

The claim would not be against the driver, but against his insurance company. Compensation claims are now a huge industry. If you go into a supermarket and a tin of baked beans falls off the top shelf and hits you, you sue the supermarket. Lawyers get rich on the process, and there is much lucrative work for their henchmen – psychiatrists, loss assessors. The purpose is to establish a financial scale to 'quantify' your injury or loss.

In spite of the confusion of my feelings at the time, I decided we would embark on a claim. It was something specific to do and should result in a sizeable award, or so I was advised.

Immediately I realized the dangers. I would no doubt have to go over and over the details of my accident. This might involve my two remaining children, and cause them emotional distress. They had quite enough to cope with anyway. Would this not be an intolerable burden for them?

And what about the money? In the strict sense I did not need the money urgently (I had a job and was able to pay my bills). My wife had wisely insured her life for just such an eventuality. Money is a symbol of exchange. Was it not just cheap to take money for what I had been forced to give up? Or was it in some sense the public acknowledgement of our loss?

On a practical level, what would I do with the money once I had received it? Give it to charity? Blow it as some kind of gesture of defiance? Buy a Lamborghini?

The compensation claim I embarked on lasted 5 years and I had at the outset no idea what it would involve. I consulted my brother-in-law, a senior partner in the law firm Farrer and Co. in London. He said his firm would be happy to act for me, but I decided that I must remain as detached as possible from this legal process and to involve any member of my family would be a mistake. I found out that the firm of Russell, Jones and Walker was expert in claims of this kind and one of its partners was put in charge of my case.

The purpose of a claim of this kind, as I have said, is to quantify loss. There are absurd aspects to this, as I shall describe. How can one quantify emotional distress? Material loss is a different matter. One of the most bizarre aspects of this was the cooperation between the legal and medical professions. Feelings of grief and bereavement are extremely complicated and as mysterious as the human personality itself. But in order to quantify the emotional distress all three of us had suffered, I had to be examined and in some cases re-examined by psychiatrists, clinical psychologists, neurologists and neuro-psychologists – a whole battery of professionals. This is not to mention two visits to orthopaedic surgeons to examine my bones, and three visits from a personal loss assessor.

The purpose of much of the medical and psychological examination was to 'label' me. Was I now a clinical depressive? Was I so grief-stricken that I might go mad? Could I be shoved into a category which might persuade a judge to award me more money? There seemed to be some kind of scale of awards. If I had gone into the psychiatrist's clinic doing a John Cleese walk and giving the appearance of lunacy, I might get a lot more money.

All this seemed to me to be somewhat absurd. The grief and pain at our loss was something we wanted to come to terms with very privately. I did not want to be peered at and examined by a string of people who were filling in reports and passing judgement on the state of my body and my psyche. And I most certainly did not want my children to be exposed to all this either.

The person who delved into my psyche in the most irritating fashion was the neuropsychologist. His brief was to see what effect the accident had had on my own mental processes. I was submitted to more than an hour of intelligence tests (all too reminiscent of IQ tests at school, at which I was a complete disaster). At the end he drew himself up and passed judgement of my thinking processes, my power of memory and my ability to express myself in writing and in speech.

This made me furious (a fury I contained). How dare this man pass judgement on me having only met me for an hour? I stormed down Wimpole Street in a rage.

I then had a lengthy visit from the representative of an organization specializing in personal injury assessment. The purpose of this was to 'quantify' the loss of my wife in the context of our domestic and family life. I had to provide a list of every domestic activity my wife undertook.

Sarah was an extremely practical person. If there was a domestic task to be achieved or a problem to be solved, she would never call in outside help unless she had failed to solve it first herself. Her activities ranged from making curtains, plumbing repairs and gardening, to driving the children to school and organizing holidays. It also involved unblocking the loo and laying concrete slabs in the garden. In every sense, she was a strong woman.

Against every one of these activities was put a sum of money. I found this at once rather comic but also slightly insulting. But it was part of the process I had embarked on, and I had to go through with it. Certificates had to be obtained from specialists to demonstrate what outsiders would have charged for doing the jobs that my wife undertook so willingly.

Another important issue came to the fore at this stage. Four years before she died, my wife had given up a successful career as a publisher to write a novel. The book was completed days before she died and it was published posthumously under the title *Hanging On*. I now needed to demonstrate that by her death a brilliant writing career had been cut short, and we were to be deprived of much income.

The novel was published to much critical acclaim and was as commercially successful as a novel could possibly be without an author to promote it. It was pointed out to me that the nearer I could get to proving that Sarah would be the new Jackie Collins, the more money I would extract from the insurers.

The reviews were plentiful and favourable. Rabbi Lionel Blue selected it as his book of the year in the *Evening Standard* describing it as 'Dostoevsky with a Harrods heroine'. Sarah he described as a 'spiritual Jilly Cooper'. Nicola Beauman in her review wrote: 'the novel is marvellously entertaining. The tragedy is that the author will never have the chance to go from strength to strength – as I am sure she would have done'.

\* \* \*

By the time all this work had been done, it was the beginning of 1997. My children also had to visit the lawyers to try and quantify their loss.

It was time to visit the barrister to assess progress. I was summoned to his chambers. He was a man of courtesy and tact. During the meeting I received a devastating and quite unexpected blow. The barrister let slip that my son Archie had regained consciousness after the accident. I felt pole axed.

In coming to terms with my loss, I had been reassured by the certainty that Archie had died without suffering any pain. Now I learned after 3 years that this was not the case. My lawyer, perfectly reasonably, told me that she had not mentioned this to me in order to save me distress. This new knowledge released in me a severe depression from which it took me some weeks to recover. The truth was that the shock of the accident was beginning to wear off and I felt worse than I had ever felt since the accident itself.

A definition of depression is 'anger turned in on oneself'. As the depression lifted, I managed at last to feel real anger and came to realize that the compensation claim was serving a useful purpose therapeutically as an outlet for my anger. If it was a case of arguing about pounds, shillings and pence, so be it. I was going to go for every penny I could get. At this stage the insurance company made an offer for the loss of my son, Archie. This was £12,500. My barrister advised that we should accept, as the much bigger issue, financially speaking, was the loss of my wife. He may have been right, but this kind of logic was fairly unreal to me. It all pointed up the absurdity of awarding money for life.

I then went back for a second series of examinations by the medical professionals that I had seen first time round. I seemed to come out with fairly good marks. 'Mr Baird-Smith is coping very well'. 'Mr Baird-Smith has adjusted very well to his new life'. More judgements passed on me by outsiders who knew so little of what I and my children were really feeling. In order to cover up my distress and survive, I was determined to put on the appearance of being cheerful and optimistic, in part at least as a defence mechanism against what was really going on inside me.

By the end of 1998, a sum of money had been proposed by the insurers as a payment for the totality of my claim. After a certain amount of coming and going, my barrister advised that the proposed sum was fair and if we proceeded to trial it would be extremely expensive and we might come away with less.

A deal was agreed. I imagined that this would be the end and that I could now get on with my life. However, the lawyer told me that the settlement would have to be ratified by a judge in court, but this I gathered would be something of a formality.

I was summoned to the High Court in Holborn on a dull day in January 1999, almost exactly 5 years after the date of my accident. I had imagined that I would simply be ushered into a small room with two barristers for the formality of signing some papers. And that would be it.

We were kept waiting for an hour. The courts were running late. A previous case was running overtime – a woman was suing East Sussex Health Authority for irreparable damage done to her daughter during childbirth in an NHS hospital.

When I got to the court room, it was full of people. Worst of all, and contrary to all my expectations, there was a press box full of journalists.

Although the case had to all intents and purposes been settled in advance, the judge gave my barrister quite a hard time. As I sat at the back of the court, I listened to other people discussing my accident, talking about my wife and my son as if I was not there. Finally the judge got up, offered me his condolences on behalf of the court and said that he thought my children and I had survived the accident admirably. He then walked out.

The next day the *Times* carried an account of the case and announced to the world the sum of money I had been awarded (£145,000). My local paper, the *Hampstead and Highgate Express* carried a much longer half-page report, containing some inaccurate details.

And so the case was settled. Five years had come to a completion.

As I walked out of the High Court into Fleet Street, I felt quite alone. The encircling gloom was great. A link with the past was cut off. As the process had developed over the years, I had slowly learned to feel a bit of the anger within me, but I had some way to go.

\*     \*     \*

The weeks following the end of the court case were dark weeks. Max had gone back to university. Leonora was in Australia for her gap year. But I am a good actor and nobody really noticed. I just became rather silent.

Out of the blue, a relative and good friend of mine, Margie, called and invited me to go to Mexico with her. I had never been to Central America before. I agreed. I could get away, have a change of air. As the departure day loomed, I thought of pulling out. I didn't think I'd make it. I was not in good spirits. But I went.

The house we stayed in was at Tepozlan, on the road from Mexico City to Cuernavaca. The setting was extraordinary. The colours were vibrant, the surrounding mountains exceptionally beautiful.

One morning while I was there, an extraordinary thing happened. As I was sitting alone in the garden having breakfast, I felt my whole body shake. Every bone and every sinew seemed to vibrate. Behind it was a feeling of extraordinary anger. It lasted only two or three minutes. It was in no sense a spiritual experience. It was purely physical. When the shaking stopped, I felt better. A deep feeling of anger, of rage had been released. It was no longer repressed. I had no doubt that it was fundamentally an anger at the death and loss of Sarah and Archie. At last, after 5 years, it had surfaced.

But at whom was this anger directed? It had to have an object. I had feelings of guilt about the past but I was not angry with myself. How could I feel anger against the driver who had driven into me? I learned subsequently that his girlfriend who was in the passenger seat had suffered far worse and longer lasting orthopaedic injuries than me.

No, my anger was quite plainly directed at God. It had no other object.

I remembered that when I had read Richard Marius's magnificent biography of Martin Luther, there was a passage where the author described Luther's rage against his father. It was a rage so brilliantly described that I felt it in my guts. That was the nearest I had ever been before to a sensation in any way similar to what I had just experienced.

One of the things I have learned from my Jewish friends and from the Old Testament is that life is a running battle with God. We should complain. We should express our anger. 'Why do the wicked prosper?' shouts Job, shaking his fist at heaven.

I find no help in that strand of Christian thinking which says that suffering is good for the soul. I prefer Bob Dylan's remark delivered with irony: 'Pain sure does bring out the best in people, doesn't it'. Or my tutor at Cambridge, Donald Mackinnon, who simply stated: 'Pain never ennobled anyone'. They may not be right, but it is bracing to read.

The French have a phrase which sends a shiver down my spine. It is 'la belle souffrance'. It was a phrase Marshall Petain used during the war when trying to persuade the French people to knuckle down under the Nazi occupation. Their temporary suffering would be for the greater glory of La Patrie – the French Fatherland. It was a form of emotional blackmail.

No, we should not take things lying down. 'Gird up thy loins', says God to Job. 'Gird up thy loins like a man. For I will demand of thee. And answer thou me'. That last phrase has a special significance for me. God commands us to grow up and answer back. There is an answer within us, and He needs to know what it is.

This is what the Swiss Protestant theologian, Lytta Basset, has called Holy Anger, Holy Rage. It is an anger that we need to learn to work with. Anger that grows from pain obliterates pain, but anger *against* pain can be anger against the self and this is destructive.

This anger I felt was almost a kind of primal energy. I felt more myself, less intimidated, more what I wanted to be. And as to God, we must never sentimentalize Him or subjectivize Him.

And it was therapeutic. When Bruno Bettelheim was working with Holocaust survivors after the war he said simply: 'My job is to help the patient feel anger'. That made sense to me.

I appreciated the remark of a rabbi friend of mine. When I asked him what he thought it would be like when we get to heaven, he just said: 'God will have a lot to answer for'.

God purifies by rage.

From time to time since then, the feelings of anger have returned to me. When it returns, I feel it. I need to feel its surge and keep on feeling it.

This is a kind of anger which is positive and even creative. It can become a powerfully creative force. Maybe it is part of God's creative activity within us.

The novelist Muriel Spark was sometimes moved to her greatest creativity by anger. When she learned that a former lover had sold her love letters at auction, she made him a central character in her novel *A Far Cry from Kensington*. In the novel she massacred him, tore him to shreds. It was one of her most successful works of fiction.

As the years advance (it is now 17 years since Sarah and Archie died) and as I have moved into a new life, with new relationships, new projects, feelings of gratitude grow in me which ultimately will be stronger than the feelings of anger. Not all anger is good. It can restrict and contract the soul, confine the heart.

The first line of the 'Magnificat' grows on me all the time. 'My soul *magnifies* the Lord'. In response to God's surprises, Mary's heart expanded, expanded with gratitude.

I was married for 18 years. I was Archie's father for 14 years. My children are both married. I have a grandson. Have I not much to be grateful for?

Let me end by turning again to Laurence Whistler. In that same book, *The Initials in the Heart*, he wrote this: 'Stranger than all misery, with its harrowing sense of short measure, is the perception I always have – have now, as I had then – of an unexpected, measureless, laughably undeserved, good fortune'.

That's it. That's it exactly.

Books referred to in the text:

C. S. Lewis, *A Grief Observed*, Faber 1966.

Laurence Whistler, *The Initials in the Heart*, Rupert Hart Davis 1968.

Anton Chekhov, *Lady with Lapdog and Other Stories*, Penguin 1969.

Sarah Baird-Smith, *Hanging On*, Constable 1995.

Richard Marius, *Martin Luther*, Harvard University Press 1999.

Lytta Basset, *Holy Anger*, Continuum 2008.

Muriel Spark, *A Far Cry from Kensington*, Constable 1988.

# CHAPTER NINE

# *Jimmy*
## Barry Mizen

*Barry Mizen is a father of nine who runs his own shoe-repair business in Sidcup and lives in southeast London with his wife, Margaret. His son Jimmy was murdered in 2008 at the age of 16.*

Jimmy would usually have been working with me on a Saturday in the shoe-repair shop I've had for 25 years, but 10 May, 2008, was the day after his sixteenth birthday so I had let him have the time off. The evening before he had gone out with his friends to cele-brate, but not before he came into the kitchen, in the new clothes we'd given him, and we'd had a three-way cuddle by the cooker, Jimmy, my wife Margaret and me. We often do that sort of thing in our house. We told him how proud we were of him, and he said the same to us. That was my last contact with Jimmy.

When people ask me what Jimmy was like, I often find myself saying he was lovely, but that doesn't describe him adequately. He came second-to-last among our children. We have seven sons and two daughters. He was also our second youngest son. In a big fam-ily you can almost get lost, but Jimmy didn't. He got on very well with everyone, with babies as much as adults. He was very non-judgemental but had within him a strong sense of right and wrong. I was a school governor at Jimmy's school, for example, and there was a boy there who had been excluded for the day. Jimmy came home when he learned about it and said, 'dad, that boy's innocent. You have to go and sort it out'.

Jimmy was very decent. I always remember when other boys were going out with him, their parents would say, 'oh, if Jimmy Mizen's going, you'll be alright. You're in good company'. He was very protective of his friends. He was tall, over 6 feet, and saw himself as a leader, but in the best possible way.

After his death so many people spoke of the way he was always smiling, something I took for granted, without realizing the impact it had on others. Jimmy was an amalgam of his older brothers and his nephew, who just happened to be three years older, a little piece of each of their characters was in him, facial expressions, words, way of talking and moving. He loved, and was proud of his family. Jimmy was an uncomplicated person. What you saw is what you got; I can never recall him being miserable or sulking. He had a boldness that was endearing.

I drive to and from work in a camper van and when Jimmy was with me on the journey home, we used to have our own little ritual. We'd both try to whistle the 'Sailor's Hornpipe', but we could never get through it without bursting out laughing. It was like that between us. We had our in-jokes. I have a bank of trivial jokes that each one of my children has heard over the years, and when one of them says, 'dad, you've told it before', I would say 'well you may have heard it before, but there is always another child who hasn't'. However, with Jimmy you could refer to the same jokes over and over again and he would still find them funny. Small things, but these are the memories I treasure.

Jimmy was a very practical person. He liked school, but he didn't like schoolwork. He had a statement of special educational needs and required that little bit of extra help, but away from the classroom he was very good at taking things apart and mending them,

# Jimmy

or painting a room, or putting up the Christmas decorations. Once an idea was in Jimmy's mind, he had to do it. So if you said, 'Jimmy in five years we are going to take you to Australia', he'd be wanting to pack his bags straightaway. He had this habit, if he walked into a room, when Margaret and I were half way through a conversation, of interrupting and saying, 'what's that all about, then?'

That Saturday was his last weekend before he took his GCSEs. He had a job lined up. The previous year he'd done work experience. 'Whatever I do', he told me, 'I have to go there on a train otherwise it isn't proper work'. Walking there wouldn't have been good enough. So, through a friend of Margaret's sister, we got him a couple of weeks with a property maintenance company a few miles away. They sent him out with a fitter, repairing doors, bathrooms, that kind of thing. This chap was, by all accounts, sullen – 'I don't want a kid with me' and the rest of it – but by the end of two weeks Jimmy had bowled him over. So much so that they created an apprenticeship for him. And this in a firm that had never had apprentices before.

There was a teaching assistant who knew Jimmy when he was in primary school. This lady has a choice way with words, but she said something about him that often comes back to me. 'There's not a brat bone in his body.' And that was Jimmy to a T. He was very straightforward.

I was at work in my shop in Sidcup on that Saturday morning in May 2008. I had had an awkward customer in. We couldn't find her shoes and she got quite confrontational, so I missed the phone the first time it rang. Second time, I picked it up and it was Margaret screaming, 'get here quickly, Jimmy's been attacked in the bakers'. So I just left the shop and drove the 5 miles home. It was The Three Cooks' Bakers, just round the corner from where we live in Lee. I remember I had such a strong sense of foreboding. As I drove, I prayed all the way, over and over again.

103

When I got near, all the roads were closed and the traffic was backed up. I knew a side road, so I did a U-turn and ended up just leaving the van in a friend's drive. She was outside wondering what all the fuss was about. I threw the keys at her. 'It's my son', I said, and went running down towards the bakers.

I remember seeing Margaret running towards me. There were emergency vehicles, police, ambulance, lights. The area was cordoned off with plastic tape. I started noticing people I knew, and members of my family inside the cordon on a patch of grass opposite the bakers. My son, Harry, was sitting on the ground with his back against a tree, sobbing. Another son, Tommy, had his back against a low brick wall. A good friend of his was crouching next to him, comforting him. Tommy was wearing shorts and the bottom half of his body was covered in blood.

I wasn't allowed into the shop. It was a crime scene, the police said, so no one could go in, but there was a paramedic coming out, taking his gloves off, and someone saying, 'he's dead'. My first reaction to hearing that was, 'What am I supposed to do now? Am I supposed to fall on the floor? Scream and shout?' I was baffled. I just sat down on the kerb.

Subsequently we have tried to piece together what happened. Jimmy and his brother, Harry, had gone out that morning, stopped off in the newsagents to buy Jimmy's first lottery ticket and a paper, and then walked into the bakers. While they were waiting their turn, Jake Fahri had come in. He was 19 at the time and lived with his family very near to us. There was a history. When Harry had been in year seven at school, Jake, from another school, had mugged him for 20 pence. We notified the school and they said they'd spoken to him, he was sorry, it wouldn't happen again.

A couple of years later, Harry had been getting off a bus and Jake was there. 'You're the one who grassed me up', he said and beat

Harry up. He had come home very distressed, so we contacted the police. They spoke to Jake and his parents and then came round to our house and told us that Jake and the Fahris were very, very sorry. It wouldn't happen again.

By May 2008 Jake was a known thug in the area, involved in drugs, with previous convictions. He came into the shop and told Jimmy and Harry to 'get out of the f***ing way'. Jimmy – and this was his character, his decency – turned round and said to Jake something along the lines of 'some manners wouldn't go amiss'. So Jake then said to Jimmy, 'Do you think you're a big man?' Jake is short and Jimmy was tall. 'Come outside and I'll show you'. Jimmy said he didn't want a fight but Jake went out to wait for him.

Then Harry got on the phone to his brother, Tommy, for help, but Jake came back in the shop. 'Who are you on the phone to? I remember you, you're the one who grassed me up', he said and started jabbing keys at both their faces to provoke them. Then he picked up a couple of plastic drinks' bottles out of the cabinet and started banging both of them over the head with them. That was when they did react and bundled him out of the shop. They held the glass door shut from the inside.

This all comes from eyewitnesses' reports. Jake then picked up a sign outside the bakery. It had a concrete base and he used it to smash his way back through the door. Jimmy and Harry retreated behind the counter, but Jake – who one witnesses said by now had completely lost it – followed them. He picked up a glass Pyrex dish full of sausages and threw it at Jimmy with so much force that it shattered on impact. A piece of the glass was embedded in the wall 2 metres up. That is the amount of force he used. And a piece of the glass went into Jimmy's neck, partially severing his jugular vein, completely severing his carotid artery and embedding itself in his spine.

Jake then ran out of the shop. One of the witnesses said she saw him running up the road laughing. Three days later he would give himself up to the police.

Tommy by this time had turned up and Jimmy, even though he was bleeding badly, had run to the back of the shop in fright and shut himself in a cupboard. Tommy followed the trial of blood but Jimmy was holding the cupboard door shut, thinking Jake had come back for him. Finally Tommy got the door open. Jimmy, he said, looked terrified, but recognized him, and collapsed into his arms. It was Tommy who cradled him while he died.

People were screaming, 'get an ambulance,' and Tommy was pressing tissues against the wound to try and stop the blood, but we were told later that the wound was such that nothing could be have been done to save Jimmy. The fear he must have felt still causes us great pain, the same fear we saw on his face when we viewed him in the public mortuary 2 days later.

What I do remember of that moment was how quiet it was there, and how it suddenly went very cold. That may just have been my body reacting, but others said later that the quiet was tangible. And then it was all people and phone calls. Danny, our oldest, was on a rugby tour in Spain. A couple of the others were away working. They all made their way back.

The next day was Sunday and we went to mass at 9 o'clock as we always do. Everyone was crying. I was down to be the Eucharistic Minister that day, and wanted still to do it. I was holding the chalice at Holy Communion time and people were coming up to me weeping. My shirt was wet through with their tears. Yet I was so calm. It was strange. At that mass, I kept thinking, it should be me crying and other people comforting me.

Traumas happen in everybody's life. We have a daughter, Samantha, for example, who has Downs' Syndrome. When she was born, it was traumatic, but we have coped and she is a dear, sweet, much-loved part of our family. And when you look back, you wonder how you coped, but all you know is that you did. There is something that enables each of us to cope with the traumas that come our way. What that something is is for each person to decide. Margaret and I would say it is our faith.

I remember subsequently meeting Richard Taylor, whose son Damilola had been killed in 2000 in Peckham. It was 7 years then since Damilola's murder but Richard said, 'I'm sorry to add to your burden but I still cry, even after all these years'. That helped us as we prepared to deal with our loss. He is now a dear friend, as are a lot of other families who have lost a loved one to violent crime. The support and understanding we all receive from each other is so welcome and needed. People talk a lot about closure after a death. I think it's because they want everything to be all right again, for you to 'get over it' so they can feel better. I don't want closure as, in a way, it will be like shutting something out of my life. What happened is part of who I now am, and I have had to learn to live with that. When someone is ripped out of the heart of a family in the way Jimmy was, it redefines you as a person. I am now a different person to the one I was.

From the start, I was also very, very determined that I would not be beaten by Jimmy's death. I've reiterated it time and time again in the years since, usually when I am overcome thinking of him. That was a conscious decision, an effort. I absolutely refused to show any emotion in public. People at the time described Margaret and me as 'dignified' because we didn't break down and cry in public, but in private, at night-time, when it is so painful you can't sleep, we were awake, crying our eyes out, holding each other.

I remember in particular something said to me by a friend who had lost a son to 'sudden adult death syndrome'. 'You've got to hold it together for the rest of the family. It is your responsibility.' And he was right. That's not to say that everyone else in the family wasn't trying to do the same, but I saw it as my responsibility as Margaret's husband and their father.

Again, people who saw Margaret and me on television, speaking about Jimmy's death, said, 'you were so together', and we were, but that wasn't because we'd planned it, it is just how we were, how we are. We agreed to talk to the media quite early on. I know what the media can do and I didn't want my family or Jimmy to be portrayed in any bad way. Every few months in the papers there will be a big family shown as a bunch of scroungers. We are a big family, but I was determined that people should know the truth about us and about our son. And we remain grateful that is what happened.

Jimmy's death still causes me to reflect on how we brought up our children. We live in a big city and I was always sure that I wanted to make my children street-wise because of the things they were going to be confronted with out there. But we never taught them to get the first kick in. We've never taught them that, if someone hits you, you hit them back. Those are some of the values we have tried to live by as a couple, as a family, the values we have instilled in our children. Yet part of that, after Jimmy's death, has been asking myself should I have taught him to be more aggressive, as some parents do, and if I had, would he still be alive today? Maybe Jimmy's backing away from confrontation that day in the bakers was seen as a sign of weakness by the bully and that encouraged him to push it further? Bullies, after all, get off on exerting power over other people. But then Jimmy had this sense of what was right, these values, and he stood up for them. If we had brought him up differently as a family, if Margaret and I had taught our children to be aggressive and physically confrontational, then this family would a different one from what it is, and I don't want that. My children are laid-back, decent and sociable – that is what people tell us.

We had a memorial service for Jimmy a week after he died. Margaret and I went over to talk to the press afterwards. I realize now that many families don't get that sort of attention, that sort of platform, but at the time you have no perspective. It was just some thing that was there, and so we spoke. We didn't want Jimmy's death to be used by politicians for a knee-jerk reaction to issues of violence, by bringing in a new law. So we asked the questions that had been going through our heads – Did we really need new laws, more laws, or did we need everyone to ask what sort of society they want to live in, what sort of values they want to live by, and whether it is for each one of us to do that?

I still firmly believe that it is, and that is what has driven all we have worked towards since Jimmy's death. One of the most common things people say to us is, 'I've got a son Jimmy's age'. Before his murder, they had thought it wasn't their problem, but now, they say, they realize that issues of anger, confrontation and violence are a problem for us all. The government and police can't solve them on their own. We all have to work for a more civil, safer society in which to raise our families, based on peace and justice.

Margaret also said on that occasion that she felt such an empathy with Jake's parents. We had tried to put ourselves in their shoes – what if the police had come to our door and told us that one of our sons had killed someone. So Margaret asked the media to leave Jake's parents alone. We have such lovely memories of Jimmy, she said. We cuddled him as a baby, just as Jake's parents had cuddled their son as a baby, but what memories do they have of him now he's done this wicked thing? And those remarks were picked up and have come to define us as a family, though at the time you are totally unaware of the impact your words will have.

I knew Jake's name before he killed Jimmy, because of the bullying with Harry, but I'd never seen him. For me, now, it's almost as if he never existed. I can barely acknowledge him. Perhaps if there was a CCTV camera I could view from inside the prison where he is serving a mandatory life sentence for murder, with a minimum tariff of 14 years, it would be different. And, thank God, I have never had a sense of wanting retribution. There has been and is anger in this family. It would be wrong to pretend otherwise, but as a family we are working through it together.

Jake's family still lives close at hand. They were in the public gallery at the Old Bailey during the trial in March 2009, while we were in the well of the court. Some comments were made by members of his family – not the parents – to some of my family who were also in the public gallery, and we had to complain to the court authorities. I was proud that my sons didn't react. I do remember, when the jury was being selected, looking up to the gallery and seeing what I think was one of Jake's aunties. She was staring at me with such hatred. I have never experienced that level of hatred in a look before. I was so taken aback.

The parents have never made any attempt to contact us. I don't know what I would do if they did. And I wouldn't know them if I saw them in the street. I do, sometimes, find myself deliberately driving past their house. I don't know why. Perhaps it is some connection with Jimmy? When he was in the mortuary, before he was buried, I used to drive down there at night and sit in the car park. It was a way of being near to him. We had wanted to have a wake at our family home, with the coffin open, but we were told that the body had deteriorated to such an extent we were advised not to. That was painful.

For the family it was like a second bereavement.

When asked about how we were coping, we spoke from the beginning about our faith, but we also made a conscious decision about the words we chose. Although we are Catholics, we have never mentioned Catholicism in particular, or even Christianity – though the press has highlighted it, describing Jimmy as an altar boy. Instead, we have talked about how a religious faith, any religious faith, has a place when you are grieving. Faith, for me, means a belief that there is more to this life than what we can see. Everyone gives that belief different names, but if it makes them a person of peace, then I make no distinction. And, of course, you can be a person of peace and have no faith.

People often described Margaret and me as 'the couple who forgive'. The question comes up all the time: Do you really forgive? How can you? The answer is that it depends what you mean by forgiveness. What I mean by forgiveness is that I do not seek revenge. I am not saying what Jake did doesn't matter, but for me forgiveness is about not wanting to do to that person what he has done to me. And I say that because I realize that it is the best way forward for me. Immense damage has been done to this family by Jimmy's murder, and I have no wish to make that worse – to damage my children more, to risk breaking up my marriage – by seeking revenge and retribution. It comes back to our determination that this must not destroy us.

To that end, we made a conscious decision after Jimmy's death that we wanted some good to come out of it. A friend of ours who is a teacher in a school in Bermondsey asked Margaret and me if we would go in and talk to the children about what had happened, how we had reacted, and answer their questions. We had no idea what it would be like but we agreed. That was really the beginning of what has become the Jimmy Mizen Foundation.

It has just evolved. People have come to us and we have responded as best we can. Sometimes we have had to say no. There was one documentary maker who came to us shortly after Jimmy died and wanted to film us right through until after the trial, which we couldn't do. After the visit to the school, though, we started getting invited to other places. So we put together a short film with photos of Jimmy to show them. His brother, Tommy, composed a song. And we are still to this day talking in public about him and what happened and the need for a peaceful response.

We have always tried to make whatever invitations we accept a family decision. There was a bit of resistance at first, but, as it has evolved, everyone has grown more comfortable with it. The first practical thing came along when we got involved with the local scouts – where Jimmy used to go – and agreed to help fund a mini-bus, to be called a 'Jimmy Bus', with money that some student friends of Harry's had sent us after a whip round. Then we were doing an interview with a national newspaper, mentioned the 'Jimmy Bus', and people started sending us cheques and notes and coins. We have ended up with two Jimmy buses, and are adding a third.

Then the firm that Jimmy had been going to join as an apprentice after his GCSEs wrote and said that 'Jimmy showed us the potential of young people', so they still wanted to take on two young lads but intended to call them 'the Jimmy Mizen Apprenticeships'. We wanted to see if we could promote more of these initiatives.

And from there, it has grown. We have worked with London Citizens and the Metropolitan Police on a scheme called 'City Safe', and now the Mayor of London and other cities are picking up on the initiative. We are involved with awareness-raising in schools and, through a charity called The Forgiveness Project, have been visiting prisons and prisoners, telling them our story and what we have tried to do since Jimmy's death. Recently we opened the Café of Good Hope in Lewisham, run by some of Jimmy's brothers, to raise funds for the foundation, and raise awareness. One day, I'd love to have enough to buy the Three Cooks' Bakers, where Jimmy died, and turn it into another café, or even a garden in memory of him.

A few months before he died, two girls in the same year at Jimmy's school died in a road traffic accident. After the funerals, which they attended, the pupils had talked to each other about their own mortality, and what they would like people to say about them after they died. We were told by some of Jimmy's friends after he died that his wish had been, 'I just want to be remembered'.

There are times when I still feel him in the house, when he still is close. And others when I don't. We have pictures of him around the house, and his things. The GCSEs he never took were awarded to him on teachers' assessments. He got his five A to Cs, and an A in RE. We went to collect the certificates. I still have some of his coursework where he was writing about the Ten Commandments. There, in his writing, is 'Thou shalt not kill', and after it, Jimmy had written, 'but unfortunately sometimes people do'.

Some things in our family home have changed since he died. The sofa in the sitting room, the last place he sat before he went out that Saturday morning, had to go. Margaret couldn't bear it being there. Most of all, though, Jimmy lives on in my heart, but I live in constant dread of losing that. There is a physical pain that goes with grief. For me it is as if I have been folded in half and put in a vice. The pain wells up in my stomach and it hurts so much that I double over. But I don't get that pain as often now which should be a good thing, but it worries me. It is as if the easing of that physical pain means that I am losing my contact with Jimmy. I suppose that it was inevitable that the space between us would widen after the first weeks and months, but I don't want it to widen any more.

# CHAPTER TEN

# *Cosmo*

## Richard Davenport-Hines

*Richard Davenport-Hines is an award-winning writer and historian. His books include an acclaimed biography of the poet, W. H. Auden. His younger son Cosmo died at the age of 21 in 2008.*

The first time I saw Cosmo, on 14 June 1986, he was a few seconds old, still attached to his umbilical cord, lying on a couch in West London Hospital, and looking quietly at his new world with what seemed to me then the most gentle, quizzical smile. I could write 50 pages celebrating how loving, how zestful, how brave Cosmo was. Above all, he was the gentlest person I have known.

Cosmo was gorgeously sensual: Jenny, his mother, and I remember his bliss on eating his first strawberries, his rapture when he was swimming in lakes or seas, his exultant gratitude when his grandmother took him on Caribbean holidays. He loved sun, beaches, water, exotic food, colours and scents. When he was 3 months old, perched on Jenny's lap in a Brittany bistro, he stretched out a little arm, and tried to clutch and eat one of her *moules marinières*. After that, she and I nicknamed him 'The Moules Stealer'.

For weeks before any holiday, every one of which delighted him, little Cosmo would come into bed with us each morning, snuggle between us, plan each day of the holiday – for he was the cuddliest, giggliest, most tactile child. When he was three and a half years old, we went for Christmas to Disneyworld in Florida. I am so grateful we did this, for it has left Jenny and me with a host of joyous memories. Before the Florida trip, he studied the Disney catalogue for days, planning what rides he would take, in which order.

His favourite of all was going to be the aerial ride in 'Dumbo the Flying Elephant' carousels. His restrained excitement, but unalloyed joy, when he went on the ride with Jenny, while I watched, is one of the precious memories of my life. She and little Cosmo used to sing together a gleeful tune with their own modifications: 'Dumbo the Elephant went to town, and said goodbye to the circus . . .'

Ten days after he died, I asked Jenny to sing this song again, which she did almost with jubilation, remembering her happy day in Florida, and then fell fast asleep. I went to the bathroom, and alone there, in a house where everyone else was exhausted by grief, and deafened to further tears, I sobbed more long and terribly than I have before or since. Every month, now, I travel on trains that halt at DisneyEurope. I love seeing the tired, happy children, and crave that the parents realize how precious and fleeting are the years when their children are small, imaginative and bubbling with fun. It is a golden time, but it does not endure.

The moment of highest transcendent happiness of my life was a sunny afternoon in Anjou, while picking blackberries with Cosmo when he was 7. His joy, his eagerness and his awareness of how happy he was making me were palpable. As a little boy he loved cooking scrumptious breakfasts, laying the table with exquisite elegance, and saying with mock-complacence afterwards, 'Ahh, sim-ple luxury.' All through his childhood he adored what he called, with another mocking mispronunciation, 'shop – ping!' He didn't want expensive presents (he was never mercenary, calculating or acquisitive), but he loved household shopping, and browsing in shops with pretty, colourful things. When Cosmo was 4 years old, he was proud of a walking-stick with a dog's head handle, and used to parade with it in Kensington High Street, in yellow waistcoat, jacket and tie with a flamboyant ornamental handkerchief. 'I noticed some people laughing at me today: do you think perhaps my tie and waistcoat clashed?'

Each year's birthday was a day of grateful joy. When he was 5, as his party was ending, a public firework display was let off nearby. He adored fireworks, and when the display ended, he said demurely, 'Thank-you; but how did they know it was my birthday?' The birthday picnics, with hide-and-seeks and chases, which we used to have with his friends in Burnham Beeches, where he had favourite ponds with frogs and ducklings, are also priceless memories. With other children, he was observant, considerate and full of imaginative sympathy – and always raising laughter.

Jenny instilled Cosmo with her passion for dogs. When we bought a puppy, a black pug called Nero, 9-year-old Cosmo gave a great sigh of satisfaction: 'Ah! the culmination of five years of work!' After Cosmo's death, Nero kept going round the house, nudging open doors with his snout ('Mr No-Nose', Cosmo used to call him), sniffing round rooms, trying to puzzle where Cosmo had gone. Before Nero, Cosmo had a menagerie of toy basset-hounds and stuffed bulldogs, called Snuffles, Humph and Tuck, each of which had a distinct character and temperament, and inspired a daily whirl of fantastical, teasing jokes. Cosmo's imaginary world of bassets and bulldogs, and the real love of pugs which he shared with Jenny, was so playful, intimate and loving. It must seem trite to outsiders, and yet it feels profoundly important to me.

Cosmo was a teacher's pet of the best sort: a class favourite because he was so amusing, responsible and intelligent. On his third birthday, after he danced ring-a-ring-a-roses in the red shoes of which he was so proud, his teacher said to me, 'I'll never have again quite such a delicious child – Cosmo's going to be my special one always.' When at the age of 8 Cosmo left Bassett House School, his head-mistress, who was retiring too, told Jenny, 'In all my years of teaching I don't remember any other child whom I never heard say – or do – an unkind thing.'

After he died, Sarah, who had been his first-form teacher at Westminster Cathedral Choir School, wrote to us: 'I do not remember many of the other boys, but Cosmo I never forgot. Cosmo was a favourite of mine with his clever, dry humour, his old-fashioned warmth and good manners. He did all his tasks with a ready amenability and good humour. He had a warm personality and a kind word for all; in essence he was a gentle boy.'

And Alastair, who taught him English at Bedales and became a superb friend to him, told us, 'Cosmo provided, for me, nothing but wit, laughter and lovely enjoyment', and for fellow pupils, 'liveliness, sweetness, comfort, protection and inclusiveness.' Cosmo acted in Alastair's school productions, stayed with him each summer at a house near Vezelay, revelled in Alastair's erudite gaiety and impish theatricality.

From their earliest years, Jenny read aloud at bedtime to Cosmo and Hugo, his brother. Cosmo was exhilarated by fine writing, and became a voracious, discerning reader. He developed a pithy, ironical way of talking and writing which was always lucid and light. He had a knack for using an unexpected word or outlandish phrase that somehow clinched his point unforgettably. His enthusiasm for literature inspired his friends to read novels and poems that otherwise they would never have sampled.

People lose their children as they grow up. The captivating, cuddly little boy, whose parents and stuffed toys are the centre of his life, turns into an independent young man who belongs to his friends, and cares most what they think of him. Jenny and I wanted to be unselfish and gracious as this happened: we had seen the ugliness of parents who will not relinquish control, but scheme to remain centre-stage in their children's lives.

Cosmo changed after he turned 17, in 2003. Until then, he had seemed not only incisively intelligent but ambitious, focussed and with a tactical sense in his life. At Bedales, he had been elected to the school council in his first year. He was then small and skinny compared with other boys (although to his delight he later grew to 6 foot 2 inches), and made himself conspicuous as a campaigner by wearing a tee shirt blazoned 'Nobody knows I'm a lesbian'. He was on the editorial board of the *Bedalian* from early on. He had already several contemporaries or relations who were expensively educated, clever, rich but too complacent, self-conscious, indulgent or timid to try hard or compete for life's prizes. He wrote a coruscating article for the *Bedalian* about spoilt children who did not know their luck or exert themselves.

My hope, which I hardly hinted, was that he would go to work in an auction house, or a Cork Street art gallery, for he had a keen eye for appraising and arranging objects – part of the natural balance with which he saw the world – and an easy, smiling charm which would have made him a winner in that smooth world. My friend Miranda, who met him just once, at my fiftieth birthday party when he was 17, wrote to me: 'Your Cosmo seemed so golden, so blessed, that everyone who knew him has carried this lovely image, like a perfect miniature, a kind of hearthold. He'll always be there for me, as he was that night at the Ritz, a lovely, graceful, charming boy.'

I suspect that Cosmo's visual and auditory hallucinations began while he was touring in the summer of 2003 during his eighteenth year. On New Year's Day of 2008 (five months before he died) he wrote with cryptic hope: 'I feel sharper and more in control than I have for 5 years since Baden-Baden & the shroom induced death of the brain boy.' In the autumn of 2003, he abandoned the school council and newspaper, and diverted his ambitions. He felt to me a different person. In the last year of his life, I said to him shyly, trying not to show my disappointment, 'You changed a great deal, suddenly, when you were 18. What happened?' He gave me an astounded look, and said with a wary smile, 'However did you know? Yes, something did happen in my last year at school, but I can *never*, *never* tell you what it was.' I thought it might have been sexual, and was keen not to pry: with stupid, misplaced tact I asked no more.

Music became indispensable to Cosmo. 'I'm going to the greatest lyricist of my generation', he promised Jenny. He wrote songs, played the guitar and harmonica in clubs, and plunged into the London music scene. He had good friends there: Pockets, Luis, Will and countless others. Some of his lyrics were promising, but latterly I found them intolerable – the words confused or meaningless – his voice when he sang sounding anguished to me. This increasingly distanced us; and now I envy Jenny, who appreciated his efforts and was never estranged from him. I risk offending his friends by admitting that I feel that his musical obsessions were central to his madness.

Cosmo went to read English literature at King's College, London, and his tutors there have told me that he was a brilliant pupil in his first two years. His zest, his piercing intuitions, his leadership among his contemporaries, the arresting and precise way he spoke, his wit – all these were for a time undiminished in seminars. Three weeks after his death, we collected his BA in a degree ceremony in the Barbican. His name was read out, and the thousands in the auditorium were puzzled as a late-middle-aged couple clambered onto the stage. 'This degree is being awarded posthumously,' added the vice-chancellor, 'and is being collected by his parents.' Jenny and I felt a rippling shock around us. Everyone in the building stood up together, stamped their feet, clapped and roared. I have never heard such a devastating noise: it was louder than a bomb.

Cosmo was not lost abruptly, but from the age of 18 he was deteriorating. Jenny and I had little sense of his illness until (after his death) I read his diaries and notebooks, which are incoherent, scarifying and so lonely. Initially we thought he had become exasperatingly zany. In his final months we were helplessly anxious. Always it was impossible to imagine that our son who had been so lucid, calm and happy was in the thrall of madness. He was never diagnosed with schizophrenia, indeed was never seen by a physician about his mental state, though he was half an hour away from being sectioned when he escaped and died.

In his year between school and university he spent months travelling alone in the United States. He sent richly funny letters to his friends from America, but I deduce from his notebooks that he was playing at being a crazy troubadour, and trying to treat his slewed perceptions as a weird gift. Back in London, he became vaguer, forgetful. His notebooks show that he believed that he had psychic powers and could mind-read strangers by staring at them.

At the age of 20 he made a secret pact with the Devil as part of an unrequited infatuation that he felt for another boy. This most streetwise of children, who had been the youngest Westminster Cathedral Choir School pupil to cross London on the tube alone after school, became a vulnerable young man, who kept getting robbed late at night, on our front doorstep, in Golborne Road, at bus stops. Street-thieves could see his vulnerability, which his family could not.

Cosmo became convinced that his destiny was to help in evolving language. He wondered 'if the words are speaking us' instead of people speaking words. He imagined 'each syllable an organism jumping from host to host'. It is a trait of his illness that vocabulary and ideas become disjunctive, confused and ultimately meaningless. Imperceptibly, at first, but ultimately with an all-destructive crash, the eloquence and originality of Cosmo's language, which had been his pride, lurched into a chaos of non sequiturs and crazy juxtapositions. Here is one example from his last diary: 'Well, I thought, Crime & Punishment on my weary head balance, if I am, well then, make the bulb go flicker when I flap hand at it. Time tick, lids dip, screw it. Light out and Sleeep but boom barm, brain barn door flung, hell catch up omnibus.'

On 17 November 2007, Cosmo started the final volume of his diary –

to stop the facts of my life being massacred without eulogy [he wrote in its first entry]. The past year of my life has been too blurry, too strange to keep apace of.'

The opening entry alludes to his auditory and visual hallucinations – 'the assortment of Ghosts who threaten to banish me to cartoon land forever' – and his resolve to conquer them: 'This sad & fated foray into Dungeons & Dragons land must end'.

Next day he records a 'paranormal daydream', and comments, 'Jeez I absolutely am some sort of wicked creature aren't I?' On 3 December his hallucinations included 'seeing Light all over the place', and extreme stuff which he wrote 'should be left unsaid even in personal diary'. He felt lost that month, but thought that his head could be 'purged' of its internal voices, and 'the process of regaining myself' accelerated, by artistic effort. 'The Imagination traps people if they don't honour it with Creations & . . . leaves you open to invasion from Alien Voices.' On 29 December he wrote: 'I trust myself enough to know that I may be destined for something greater than even my arrogant teenager could have dreamed . . . It involves duty to things/forces I don't mention.'

In January he admitted to his friend Wim that he was 'close to madness', and regretted telling another friend Lola that he had 'sold my soul ... Since then have been getting weird electric shocks down whole body'. Sometimes he tried to reason with himself: 'The Devil does not own your soul. There is no capitalism in hell.' If a person's character is formed by their memories, then Cosmo's personality was being depleted, for he could remember next to nothing of his years at Bassett House School, and when he finished his university course in March, neither could he recall his first year there.

The 'Torture voices', he recorded in February, 'tell me to do what I don't want to'. He felt bereft of his gifts, and culpable. 'Shit I've lost so much. Can't blame it all on anyone but my own self.' At the end of February the voices temporarily abated. 'Silencio seemingly. Mind peaceful. Woke convinced that future of planet earth lay in group sex.'

Cosmo became isolated because he no longer made sense when he met friends. In March he sent Sarah 'whose birthday it was a meandering text message about a mare who ate heather & went to heaven. She didn't text back. Not surprising.' He met up with his closest friend from Bassett House days, Sam, but it was not a success: he seemed so dazed and incoherent that Sam thought he had been smoking lots of dope.

Cosmo came to me one day full of excited pleasure, but I think with underlying sadness. He had just returned from Tate Modern, where by chance he had met a beautiful, brilliant ex-Bedalian, Natasha. I suspect that his talk made no sense, and he knew it. 'I was very happy to see him, but he seemed withdrawn and vague', she told us in a wonderful letter: she thought, as many did, that he had a drugs hangover from a party the night before. As they said goodbye, he told her to wait, and rifled through his bag, pulled out a battered brown envelope containing a flick comb and other miscellanea, and found a surfer sticker: 'This is for you!' She kept the sticker for weeks, and threw it away just before his death. 'He was extraordinary, and I will never forget him,' Natasha wrote. Those are just the words that one most wants to hear about a dead child, and can sometimes believe.

March was altogether a bad month. 'I have destroyed Love', he wrote. 'Unless I am careful about all that happens over the next few days, months, however long it's going to be, I will go to hell . . . I have no excuse or justification for what I have done except the voices . . . My only hope for salvation is telling the truth to the people I am close to. Only my truth is so strange I can't work out how to put it across. I am not an evil person. What I have done is chaos, created a situation so sick and evil it is senseless.' His university course effectively ended on 20 March, and two nights later he went wandering among the dead-beats of central London. His account has flashes of his old eloquence, but shows what the future of this once-brilliant boy would have been without lifelong medication:

Ended up playing harmonica with a homeless Dude called Will. He kept boomeranging into Somerfield to buy more Lambrini. He struck up conversation with a kindly town-dweller who donated cigarettes there was a shy Indian looking girl at the stop, she wore no coat despite the torrential dew & wind. So moved out of the place to some Mosh bar, started talking with a gaggle of students, one called maybe Lindzee-Mae or maybe Anna-Ray, 'You must be on LSD', she said, tried to be normal and civil to her, she wanted me as a cartoon. Went on one knee to kiss her to prove I wasn't gay, she called security had me kicked out . . . so took a left to find Will in an alcove. We hunkered down, we played harp to the lost shoals. Folded the blanket over & went to sleep, felt curiously normal lieing next to each other, tied to corporality against the elements . . . Shook awake after an hour by his friend taken to a new alcove. He realizes someone had taken his Olde English Cider, nearly hit me, looked through my backpack. Nothing there. Bought him some new ones. We sat in a lush posh soap box entrance, 5 or 6 of us, main fixture characters. Anton, his mother had been a wanted criminal and he'd gone to America, he'd grown up there a bit. He was probably most willing to talk about his past but Will kept saying you shouldn't ask too much about each other's past; it's etiquette. I should be more forceful. Balance between going odd places & not getting beaten up is a balance to be learnt. He was encased in a nylon cocoon, poking his head out to yell his ASBO status at taxi hagglers. Nikki, she was the most gentle by far, so soft & young looking. 'You're like a fish out of water', she said as I left, 'like they said I was'. She mothered them. They all mothered each other, like a pact. They rapped 'Homeless crew'. These people felt they belonged on the streets. Like me they had a hollow, a desire to be cast aside by the known warmth, to take comfort in the home sickness, nostalgia for first separation, some sort of tantric disenfranchisement from civility.

In April, though promising himself that he was 'getting well enough to go to the Caribbean at Christmas', he recorded that he was 'going Mad in the Attic', a 'potential anti Christ', and nearly killed himself on 22 April. Next day, after reading Henry James and Greek myths, he devised some crazed ideas

about separating syla(b)bles . . . All the voices in my head, the wills of those [who] know, they flash around, they send me on different routes & partly it's why I never get close to anyone or can't concentrate. It's madness in most people's book, but I know it's real . . . if I don't raise hell, hell will raise me.

My final sight of Cosmo was a fortnight before his death: he was smiling, but stood back from me, eyeing me cagily. There had been a series of incidents – a Sunday when he was scared and loving to us after a memory black-out of which he could remember nothing; an evening excursion down the Thames to the Millennium Dome when he was distracted and weird in his behaviour – which would have been clear warnings if I had not been frittering my attention on paltry nonsense.

I half-knew the gravity of his illness, but was still fixed on the child I had loved, who was cool, calm and ironical in his self-awareness. In this final talk, I tried to dissuade Cosmo from leaving on the visit to Paris which had become an obsession and proved calamitous. I felt as I spoke that nothing I said reached him, and I realize now that he was hearing louder, tyrannous voices in his brain warning against me. It felt hopeless talking: our words petered out.

Cosmo went to Paris, obsessed with finding a ring which he said he had lost there, and with it (he told other people) all his luck and happiness. He was robbed yet again after reaching Paris (his passport and his lap-top with his latest work were lost), and fetched up at the house of my brother Edward, who reported that he seemed off his head.

Then Cosmo went missing in Paris. He might have died then and there. It is a relief to us that my brother traced him to a youth hostel; if he had disappeared, or if his body had never been identified, the doubts would have been torture. Edward took him to the Consulate General, where a temporary passport was issued. On the Friday evening of 6 June 2008 Cosmo returned on Eurostar to London.

I was at our house in a remote district of southern France, and due to return to London on the Tuesday with an elderly couple who could not travel unaccompanied: the man was a week away from a diagnosis of lung cancer. I decided not to alter my travel plans, as Jenny assured me she could cope. This was a fatal choice. I was convinced by now that Cosmo was suicidal, for on Thursday he had sent me a short email with a confused description of his 'tragic pickle jaunt' to Paris which ended: 'PS: What is the best way to kill yourself?' I recited this email to Jenny, but without convincing urgency. I should have returned early: she should not have been left to cope alone.

Cosmo, I felt sure, was set on killing himself. He knew that his sumptuous creativity was irrecoverably scrambled. The last poem he wrote, around this time, begins 'It's All In My Head', and ends, 'I was meant to be a star, he said, and now I'm just an asterisk'.

With typical generosity, he gave Jenny the last present of a lovely weekend. He was quiet, loving, considerate: physically and emotionally aloof, but sweet and affectionate in his manners. She made an appointment for him to visit his physician on Monday morning – 9 June: she did not want to cause the trouble of requesting a home visit. But as they walked together to the surgery, he suddenly ignited in terror. 'You don't understand: I'm the Antichrist', he shouted, and wrestled her into fast-flowing rush-hour traffic at Shepherd's Bush Green.

They might have been killed, but the cars stopped. Passers-by made to call the police, but Jenny, who was terribly shocked, demurred, and together she and Cosmo walked home. 'I'm going to make a pot of tea', he said, and went downstairs to our basement kitchen. She went upstairs to telephone the doctor to report what had happened. It took a couple of minutes to get through. 'Where is he now?' the doctor asked. 'Making tea downstairs', she said. 'Are you sure?' the doctor asked again.

For all of Hugo and Cosmo's lives we have lived in a tall house that backs onto a railway line running north from Olympia station. When they were small, the railway was a pleasure in their lives, and a source of *cachet* with their friends. Occasionally old steam-engines chugged past. Eurostar and the chocolate-coloured Orient Express used to trundle along on their way to be cleaned. A cargo of nuclear waste, with its unmistakeable heavy rumbling, passed at the same time each night. The boys used to sit on the garden wall to watch the trains, or laugh when Nero as a puppy used to bark at the trains, and look victorious when always the carriages retreated into the distance. Hugo and Cosmo were railway children, for whom the line was a backdrop to play.

After the doctor's question, Jenny went to a window and gazed out. She saw, on the railway line, two men trudging along with a stretcher. They were moving slowly, as if they did not want to reach what they were heading for. She knew that Cosmo was dead.

He had left by the kitchen door, scrambled over the back wall, and slid down the embankment. We live just beside the Lower Addison Gardens railway bridge, which he had scurried under. There is a wall hiding the railway from passers-by in the mews beyond the bridge. He squatted beside a bush there, and as a commuter train rattled southwards he dived in front of the driver's cabin.

Cosmo was supremely gentle: he abhorred violence, rage and railing against events. He loved calm and order, which is why his illness was such anguish to him. He loved reason, irony, restraint, the emotional under-statements that constitute true sincerity. He was quick-witted, but never hurtful. Even when he was very ill, he showed terrific fear but never anger, and the only act of violence in his life, his very last act, was (so he thought in his crazed head) an act of generosity, that he was saving the world from the Antichrist.

The train utterly destroyed Cosmo. He was only identifiable by his fingerprints. Months later, the Transport Police returned some possessions to me. I keep his smart black boots, which they murmured were 'covered with residue', under my work-table and their rusty stains seem to preserve contact with him. With them I keep a train-shredded copy of Dave Eggers' novel *A Heartbreaking Work of Staggering Genius*. When Jenny and I were at the undertakers, the woman asked if we would like Cosmo dressed in any favourite clothes for the coffin. I said, 'I'm afraid there isn't enough left of him for that', and she looked at her file, and seemed to bite her lip.

Cosmo was beautiful, with gorgeous physical grace, and it is mortifying to think of him having such a death. Involuntarily I often think of the last 3 seconds as he dived beneath the train and the wheels obliterated his head. This thought greatly troubled me until I was helped by finding Willa Cather's story 'Paul's Case', which puts into soothing words a version of death by train. A young man, who once had cherished musical hopes and imagined taking exotic journeys, waits beside the railway line leading from Newark to Philadelphia:

He stood watching the approaching locomotive, his teeth chattering, his lips drawn away from them in a frightened smile; once or twice he glanced nervously sidewise, as though he were being watched. When the right moment came, he jumped. As he fell, the folly of his haste occurred to him with merciless clearness, the vastness of what he had left undone. There flashed through his brain, clearer than ever before, the blue of Adriatic water, the yellow of Algerian sands.

He felt something strike his chest, and that his body was being thrown swiftly through the air, on and on, immeasurably far and fast, while limbs were gently relaxed. Then, because the picture-making mechanism was crushed, the disturbing visions flashed into black, and Paul dropped back into the immense design of things.

My friend Douglas, whose young sister killed herself long ago, told me a wise thing. He said that when young people kill themselves, they may realize the immensity of the act, and know its violent impact, but they do not realize its finality. They do not understand that death is permanent: death goes on and on; the dead are always dead, for there is no end to being dead.

Cosmo was 5 days short of his twenty-second birthday: too young to understand his death's finality. He was deeply, terribly mad when he died – no one who has heard Jenny's account of his last half-hour can doubt his derangement – and had no sense left. Recently I entered an art exhibition which the curator had festooned with the puerile slogan, 'Madness is freedom'. I stood stock still with disgust.

Jenny is a woman with a rejoicing spirit who tries to feel grateful about everything: happiness is in her DNA. Cosmo was identical in this. She told me a few days after he died, 'I'm determined this isn't going to ruin my joy-in-life'. Reminding me of this, 2 years after he died, she added softly, 'but it has'. We are united by a crushing sense of total failure. How could we fail to protect the most precious, ingenious, beautiful thing in our lives?

Jenny has many clear memories, but mine are few, which feels like a theft. I have recurrent dreams, though, in which Cosmo sadly, gently, with a rueful smile, reproaches me for not protecting him more carefully. I always wake from these dreams, for the emotion is intense. They are poignant, but I am pleased to dream this way every month. Cosmo, whom I can only dimly conjure when I am awake, is vivid, smiling and vital in my dreams; and seems close and real afterwards.

There was a huge party with hundreds of Cosmo's friends – all in bright clothes, as we had wished – after his funeral. Two strangers, valiant and wonderful, introduced themselves as his lovers. Gentle, beautiful Charlie had tears coursing down his face, and I shall never forget our talk: Cosmo had told him a few months earlier that he loved him. Andrew, who is just as handsome, showed iron self-discipline and awe-inspiring intelligence. He and Charlie are subtle and lovely, for Cosmo had excellent taste. 'Having sex with Cosmo,' Andrew told me, 'was like going to bed with Ariel'. My son had ravishing, voluptuous looks, I think. I feel a chilling regret that he died so soon, with so much incomplete and unconsummated:

The good not done, the love not given, time
Torn off unused.

My most vivid memory from his funeral is of Jenny and me following the coffin into the church, St John the Baptist in Holland Road, where he had been baptized and where he had served as a boat-boy swinging incense. As we started down the aisle, I saw a dear school friend of Cosmo's called Louis, turn and look at the coffin, his normally merry face suddenly a rictus of horror and anguish, and he hurled himself howling into the arms of the woman next to him. I will never forget that moment.

Our organist friend, Paul, had recruited a choir who only knew that they were to sing at a young man's funeral. There was a cry of incredulous shock when they saw Cosmo's name on the order of service, for one of them, Sophie, had been at school with him. Although stunned, she sang with superb self-control. Cosmo's friend Marco was the funeral's impresario. Luis sang one of Cosmo's songs, Bel and Lucy spoke about him, Gerard recited a haunting poem that he had written in Cosmo's memory, and Gabriel read Cosmo's favourite Shakespeare sonnet. They were so brave and generous.

My second most vivid memory of the funeral was coming down from the lectern after I had spoken for 8 minutes about Cosmo. People tried to dissuade me from this speech, fearing an embarrassing breakdown, but Jenny was far wiser: 'Of course, you can do it. It's just a performance.' I am inexpressibly glad that I did it. As I came down from the lectern, I could feel the congregation – there were 300 or 400 in the church – electrified, pole-axed. This is how I ended:

Cosmo with his relish of the human comedy, his delicious sense of the absurd, his wittiness that reduced everything to proportion gave us 20 years of laughter to remember, but whether they will be enough to get us through the next 10, 20, 30, 40 years, I do not know. If some of us can promise ourselves to carry him in their hearts forever – to remember and emulate the joy-of-life, the consideration for others' feelings, the courtesy and gentleness that he personified – then his short and beautiful life will not have been a waste.

# CHAPTER ELEVEN

# *Lorenzo*

### Augusto Odone

*Augusto Odone was an economist at the World Bank in Washington when his 5-year-old son, Lorenzo, was diagnosed with ALD. He discovered a new treatment for ALD, known as Lorenzo's Oil, and celebrated in a 1992 Hollywood film of the same name. But the treatment came too late to restore Lorenzo's health. He died in 2008, aged 30.*

I still recall as clearly as if it were yesterday the scene when Lorenzo was first diagnosed. It was 1984 and Dr Donald Fishman, one of the top neurologists in Washington, came quickly to the point: Lorenzo had adrenoleukodystrophy. The diagnosis was like an unexpected violent blow. Our son, just a month away from his sixth birthday, had ad-re-no-leu-ko-dys-tro-phy! My wife, Michaela, and I thought the word sounded sinister.

Soon we realized that the condition it described was just as sinister as the word. Dr Fishman explained that ALD – as it is usually referred to – is a neurological disorder, an error of metabolism that causes degeneration of the brain. It is a rare genetic complaint, carried by the mother and affecting only boys aged between 4 and 10. It would progress rapidly, he told us, affect vital bodily functions, and within 18 months Lorenzo would be dead.

Poor Lorenzino, in a small airless room without friends, without stars, with windows that would not open, and every option slamming shut. Outside the hospital, the cherry blossoms were in full bloom. The streets were abuzz with thousands of people who had come from different parts of the United States to admire them.

We were being told to go home and watch Lorenzo die. We couldn't and didn't. We fought the prognosis. And Lorenzo lived not for 18 months but for 24 years, though within 6 months of the diagnosis our vivacious Lorenzino lay in his bed, unable to speak or move or swallow, having to be fed by a tube. Michaela, his 'Mother Tiger', believed that he still understood everything that was going on around him, that his brain was trapped inside his body, that he could feel us if we stroked and caressed him, as we did constantly, and that he could even communicate with us by moving his little finger.

He was throughout those years the calm centre of our home in Washington. His bed – and the special chair he could sit up in – was never hidden away. And he was at the centre of both our lives – Michaela's, until her death from lung cancer in 2000 – and thereafter of mine. Throughout that almost quarter of a century, his condition remained stable. It neither improved nor declined. Lorenzo was determined to live, beating off every cold, flu and even the pneumonia that the doctors feared would take him from us. He was holding his own right up to his sudden death the day after his thirtieth birthday.

I knew nothing about ALD at the start but, little by little, I began to read and learn about this sinister disease with the sinister name and its underlying causes. That is what eventually led us – despite having no medical training – to Lorenzo's Oil, a mixture of oleic and erucic acids, which can prevent the onset of the symptoms of ALD in childhood if taken early enough. The medical establishment was initially sceptical, and when our story was told in a film they accused us of preferring a 'Hollywood ending' to the facts. But an academic study recently vindicated our belief in Lorenzo's Oil, which has saved the lives of many children. Lorenzo's tragedy was that it was not available when he needed it to save him.

*

When Michaela was expecting, we spent a great deal of time going through possible names for the baby. We eventually settled on Lorenzo. The name had been in my family for generations. Indeed, all Odones come from Gamalero, a village in northern Italy. Each year on 10 August, known as the' Night of the Shooting Stars', the villagers celebrate San Lorenzo with a big feast that includes a dinner held outdoors in the main piazza. The menu includes spaghetti with boar sauce and various wines from the local vineyards. Rich and poor dance together until the small hours on a stage erected in the middle of the square.

The story of San Lorenzo, or Saint Lawrence, had struck both Michaela and me as a fitting model for our child to aspire to. San Lorenzo is one of the most important martyrs of the Catholic Church. He was captured by the Emperor Valerian on 8 August, 258 AD. The emperor asked him to divulge the names of all the wealthy Christians he knew. He had two days. Lorenzo gathered up all the poor Christians he could find. He brought them to the palace and told the emperor, 'these are the treasures of the Church'. The emperor was furious and ordered that Lorenzo be roasted on a grill.

The saint did not mind the pain. Indeed, he found the strength to tell his executioners, 'Turn me over. I am done on this side!' According to the legend, the shooting stars that fill the night sky in mid-August are Lorenzo's tears.

My Lorenzo undoubtedly had his namesake's courage, and much more besides. Before his diagnosis, I remember how Michaela thought of Lorenzo as a whirling-dervish combination of con-artistry and fair play. He dazzled people with the intensity of his small presence, and his fearless approach to life and situations. Lorenzo had always been precocious and, like his mother, had a fine ear for languages: his English was sophisticated and he often came up with words far beyond his age.

When I was posted by the World Bank to the French-speaking Comoros in the Indian Ocean, Michaela and just- three-year-old Lorenzo came with me. After a few months, he had learned French with no American accent whatsoever. Noticing a bird wandering among the bushes of our backyard, his friend Habab told Lorenzo: 'Look at how the bird is walking'. Lorenzo immediately corrected him: 'The bird is not walking, Habab, it is exploring!'

His precociousness did not stop at languages. Lorenzo liked abstract ideas. One day he was discussing with his mother the concept of void and Michaela said that one could not do anything with voids. 'Not true,' answered Lorenzo. 'You can move the cardboard tube around which paper towels are rolled, from one room to another.'

On our return to the United States from the Comoros, we lived for a while in an apartment on the outskirts of Georgetown in Washington DC. Lorenzo attended a Montessori school nearby. Soon his teachers started complaining about Lorenzo's behaviour. They said he was distracted, unruly and quarrelsome. Michaela and I could not believe that the teachers were describing our son. Then on several occasions we witnessed changes in his behaviour at home. He would have sudden tantrums and become uncontrollable. Once I was trying to teach him a puzzle game but Lorenzo, who was always so sharp, just could not get it.

Michaela and I attributed this to the move from the Comoros to Washington, and did not worry too much about it: it would take time before he would adapt, we thought. But Michaela also noticed a change in Lorenzo's speech. His crystal clear diction was now tainted with slurred words. Again we dismissed it, after suggestions that he could be copying his friends' American accent.

One day, while in his bedroom, Lorenzo lost his balance and fell on the floor. We consulted a neurologist, who ruled out any neurological problems and suggested that Lorenzo was hyperactive. That diagnosis was difficult for Michaela and me to digest. We felt strongly that Lorenzo's behaviour did not fit the profile of a hyperactive child.

Soon afterwards, we sent Lorenzo to Rosemary Hill Elementary School, not far from our house. Michaela had asked his teachers to monitor his behaviour. I drove him to school every day before going in to the World Bank. I had to accompany him to his classroom, since he did not seem able to find it on his own. When I was about to leave, he would start crying. I often had to go back to reassure him that I would return soon.

Then one day, Lorenzo told Michaela that there was a lot of noise at the school, he did not like it and did not want to go there anymore. We found this strange coming from Lorenzo. In the meantime, after careful observation, his teachers told us that Lorenzo was disorientated and often quarreled with the other schoolmates. They also suggested that he seemed to be having an auditory processing problem.

Next, Lorenzo came down with a flu. While he was recuperating, Michaela would read aloud his favourite stories. One day, while she was reading to him, Lorenzo said, 'Mommy, can you talk louder, I cannot hear you.' Michaela called me at the World Bank and told me that Lorenzo seemed to have some problem with his hearing. I was alarmed and came home immediately.

We shopped around for a hearing doctor and, when we found one, we asked him to visit Lorenzo. This revealed that there was nothing wrong with his ears, and the hearing doctor suggested having Lorenzo seen by a neurologist. That is how we met Dr Donald Fishman and eventually received the news that our son had ALD.

Sometime after his diagnosis, I took Lorenzo to a heated swimming pool in our neighbourhood. He jumped in the water but had forgotten how to swim. I had to constantly hold him and keep his head above water to make sure that he did not drink it. Back from the pool, while I was dressing, Lorenzo suddenly disappeared. I started calling his name, but could not find him. Eventually, a gentleman who was also in the dressing room of the swimming pool brought a crying Lorenzo back to me. He was completely disoriented and could not hear me.

Another heart-breaking moment came when I took Lorenzo to a football field near our house where children his age were playing a soccer match. Lorenzo wished to join them (in the Comoros I had taught him the game) but he couldn't play as his feet gave in. He started to cry and both of us were frustrated and dejected.

*

Not long after his diagnosis, his doctors suggested that we put Lorenzo on a special diet. ALD is associated with an accumulation of Very Long Chain Fatty Acids (VLCFA for short); eliminating their accumulation through a VLCFA-restricted diet might stop its progression. But Lorenzo hated the diet. In particular, he resented the limitations on the meat, especially red meat. Often Lorenzo would say, 'Papa please, couldn't I have some red meat?' When I refused, he would cry disconsolately.

That is when Michaela and I began researching – she, at the National Institutes of Health Library near our home and I, at the library of the George Washington University near the World Bank. (The Bank was kind enough to allow me to take extended lunch hours.) Each night we would discuss our findings and spark ideas off at each other. Our hope was to find a way to eliminate completely the VLCFA and therefore prevent those who carried the ALD gene developing symptoms of the disease.

The culmination of all that research and reading about scientific and medical trials came one April night in 1985 when I had an inspiration: if oleic acid, a monounsaturated fatty acid, cut in half the VLCFA, then might adding to it erucic acid – which had shown promising results when given to laboratory rats – enable us to get rid of the VLFCA altogether?

When this idea came to me, I was sitting up, keeping watch on Lorenzo. Usually it was Michaela (at first I carried on working at the World Bank, before setting up my own consultancy in Washington). She would sit there with him for hours on end, caressing him, creating a peaceful atmosphere with music, guiding the nurses who came in to help us care for him. She was a fierce Mother Tiger in refusing to allow any nurse near Lorenzo who did not treat him with gentleness and respect, and talk to him as if he understood everything they were saying. At other times, she would read to him -- introducing him, for example, to Harry Potter and eventually working their way together through the whole series.

So I consulted the three top world specialists in erucic acid: two from Canada and one from France. While the French and one Canadian were noncommittal, the other Canadian, Dr John Kramer, was forthcoming. He assured me over the phone that erucic acid had been unfairly bad-mouthed and that it would be completely safe if fed to humans. I therefore sent out a report to all researchers on ALD, proposing a therapy based on the administration of a mixture of oleic and erucic acids. Michaela found a chemist in England to put together a sample. Lorenzo's Oil was born.

I asked my sister-in-law, Deirdre, whom I afterward referred to as our favourite 'lab rat', to go on a diet using the oil. She was a carrier of ALD and the VLCFA levels in her blood were high, although not as high as those in Lorenzo. She accepted and I cooked all her foods with the oil. Since I did not want to risk losing her, I asked her to get a cardiogram every few days.

Deirdre started the diet-cum-oil regimen a few days before Christmas. After 12 days, I sent a sample of her blood to the lab to be analyzed. When I called the technician who knew about her records, he said that there had probably been a mistake: no trace of VLCFAs was found. I told him that it wasn't a mistake.

We immediately started to cook all Lorenzo's food with the oil bearing his name. After a few days, his VLCFAs came down to normal levels and his degeneration stopped. The ALD serpent that had brought so much grief to our family had been tamed for good. Since then, the oil has been administered to several hundred ALD boys and in all of them it led to normalization of the VLCFA. The preventive efficacy of the oil in asymptomatic boys under the age of 6 who carried the ALD gene was confirmed in a 2005 study by the Kennedy Krieger Institute in Baltimore. Taking Lorenzo's Oil prevented 74 per cent of the study group from going on to develop symptoms.

Lorenzo, though, had already developed symptoms before he began taking the oil. Our research had to move on to trying to find a way to reverse the damage done by ALD to his myelin sheath, the coating on the nerves that is attacked in ALD (and in adults with multiple sclerosis). To promote the work, we set up a foundation, the Myelin Project. It continues to do groundbreaking research, a tribute to Lorenzo, though I have now stood down as its president.

Its work could not go fast enough for Lorenzo. Sometimes, over the years, friends and relatives challenged us about his poor quality of life. That was not how we saw things. We continued to live in hope that the research would produce a way of restoring Lorenzo's bodily functions. It was the only thing we could do, and, in the meantime, we made sure his life was as good as it could be.

That task became mine alone in 2000 when Michaela died after her own 6-month battle with cancer. I continued, however, to be supported by Oumouri Hassane, a family friend from the Comoros who moved to Washington and was all along one of Lorenzo's chief carers.

*

Death, so long predicted, so long resisted, came quickly when it finally caught up with Lorenzo. He got the infection that killed him, I believe, through his feeding tube. For days after his death, I felt overwhelmed by huge emotions: sorrow – my son was gone; guilt – that I could somehow have prevented this; and relief – I had worried lest I die before Lorenzo, leaving my older children, Cristina and Francesco (by my first marriage), with the terrible dilemma of whether to keep their brother at home, as his parents had fought to do all his life, or to put him in a home. I knew it would be a difficult decision for them to make. Above all, Lorenzo's death brought home to me how much of my life, over the past 25 years, had been devoted to him: my focus, and inspiration, had suddenly gone

In the aftermath of Lorenzo's death, Cristina and Francesco continuously begged me to sell the house in Washington and move to Europe where they live so that I could be nearer to them. They were worried about my health, but there was more. 'You cannot go on living in the past', Cristina told me. 'You need to make a future for yourself.'

I wanted to be closer to them, of course, but I hated the idea of leaving behind our house and so many memories of Lorenzo and Michaela. On my first Christmas without him, I loathed the idea of buying a tree, since it would bring back lots of painful memories.

Passing through the room where Lorenzo lived made me very sad. There was the bed where he laid for so many years, a prisoner of his own body, the quilted covers sent to him by schoolchildren who had heard about him, and the tape recorder where we played his favourite music.

In the end, though, I agreed. Today I live in Italy, near my children and grandchildren. I try to make a future for myself, for them, but Lorenzo is always near me too. I spend most of my time writing a book about him, of which this is a first installment. I have a religious faith, but not very strong, so I don't know if I think he is in heaven, or at peace, or in the atmosphere around me. What I do know is that I dream about Lorenzo often. Sometimes he is in his sick bed, but often he is that small boy, running and swimming in the Comoros.

CHAPTER TWELVE

# *Pauline*
### Wendy Perriam

*Wendy Perriam lives in London and has published 16 novels over the past three decades, starting with* Absinthe for Elevenses *in 1980. She has also produced six acclaimed collections of short stories. Her only child, Pauline, died in August 2008 at the age of 42.*

The wind tugged at my hair as I stood at the far end of the harbour wall at Newhaven, gazing out at the expanse of open sea. In my hand was a small glass bottle, containing not a message but two letters very carefully composed. One was to my daughter, Pauline, who had died exactly a year ago, on 27 August 2008. The other was to anyone who might find the bottle, should it drift off-course, begging them to send it on its way.

Its destination was Whidby, a small island off Seattle, where Pauline, a naturalized American and married to an American, is buried. The cemetery is a beautiful, untrammelled place, lapped by waves and shaded by tall trees, but it's 5,000 miles away, so I cannot make regular visits, as I would if she were buried here in England.

Was I crazy to imagine that a small, helpless, hapless bottle could find its way down the Channel, into the Atlantic, then on to the Pacific, and eventually wash up at the Puget Sound – an interminable, unlikely journey – and not be smashed to smithereens on rocks, or blitzed by boats' propellers? Yes, undoubtedly. But I, a grieving mother, unable to visit the grave in person on this, the first anniversary, felt a deep need to reach my daughter, however irrational the means. So I asked my two grandsons, Ned and Will, to watch out for the bottle and let me know if and when it arrived, even if it took a year.

A mere two days' later, I received an email from a man holidaying in Southampton, who had found the bottle tossed back onshore and, having read my letter, sent it on its way again. The next email, a month afterwards, was in a foreign tongue. The bottle had washed up at Nazare and again been hurled back into the sea by a kindly Portuguese. The chances of my fragile little bottle travelling so far must have been a million to one, so I dared to hope that, by some extraordinary stroke of luck, it might actually reach its destination. But that was the last I heard, alas.

'Well, what did you expect?' a sceptical friend demanded. Yet, irrational or no, I intend to repeat the exercise this year. It seems important to make some gesture on every anniversary of the death; a pilgrimage to the sea and a communing with a daughter who lies cradled by another, far-off ocean. Indeed, with August fast approaching, I've already found a special bottle and written two new letters.

Letters are important. Pauline left me one to read after her death – a source of both deep sadness and deep solace – and I placed one in her coffin, reminding her that my love for her would never die. I also helped Ned compose a short note to his mother, to be placed against her heart. He and Will and I all added a small gift: Ned his favourite bear; Will a fluffy dog; I a gold-heart bracelet. Many civilisations have buried their loved ones with grave-goods and such rituals can be healing, in that part of us now lies with them, in their final resting-place.

Pauline also left letters for her sons, and we worked on these together in the last stage of her illness. She wanted the boys, then aged 10 and 7, to have a written testimony of her love for them; fearing that, as they grew older, their memory of her might fade. I suggested she tell them about their births, since, once she was no longer there, no one else would know the details. Their father, her first husband, had already died at 42, of a massive heart attack. I hoped they might find it comforting to read how overjoyed she was to hold them in her arms for the first time.

Of course, I was remembering *her* birth, and my own elation when my longed-for baby was delivered safe and well. My triumphant smile seemed to spread through my whole body and send champagne bubbles frisking through my bloodstream; a smile meriting a plinth and a glass case. An excessive reaction, maybe, but then I'd been told in my early twenties that I would never have a child and, although, in fact, I did conceive, I lost the baby at 12 weeks. After severe, protracted pain, I was finally whisked to hospital, where, due to a shortage of beds, I was placed on a trolley in a corridor and eventually miscarried in more or less public view. The hospital asked if they could keep the foetus for teaching purposes and I willingly agreed. Any chance of further 'life' for my firstborn was preferable to it being flushed unceremoniously down a sluice.

Although told I'd never conceive again, I found I was pregnant just a few months' later. However, at the critical 12-week stage, I suffered a haemorrhage and was informed by the obstetrician that the foetal heart had stopped beating – my baby was dead. My mother, a devout Catholic, stormed heaven for a miracle and, incredible as it sounds, the foetal heart re-started, two days later.

The problems weren't yet over, though. Throughout the pregnancy (much of which I had to spend in bed), the baby never kicked or made the slightest movement. In those pre-scan days, all my mother could do was continue praying – this time, that the child wouldn't be born deformed or paralysed. Hence my joy on 31 December 1965, when Pauline was delivered by the same, now tetchy obstetrician (irked at missing his New Year's Eve party) healthy, happy and very much alive. No wonder my Hosanna smile stretched from John O'Groats to Land's End.

Flash forward 42 years. I am in another hospital, sitting at my daughter's deathbed. The palliative nurse, Alicia, explained that Pauline could still hear, although she couldn't speak or move, and that *my* voice was the one she knew the best, having listened to it in the womb. Alicia said that those about to die tend to travel back in time, embarking on a 'life-review', and often starting with the first moments of existence. She suggested that we contribute to the process by telling Pauline about her actual birth. Her father and I took it in turns to recreate the saga and, although we were speaking softly, I had a sense she understood and was maybe even comforted.

All of us present in the room did our best to support her as she slipped, alone, into that 'undiscovered country'; tried to make her feel that, however terrible the parting, she was surrounded by our love. This was no time for selfish grief. Earlier, I had sobbed so hard, I felt I was being torn apart, and the phrase 'a broken heart' seemed to move from metaphor to a reality of desolation. But, as Pauline approached the moment of death, such outbursts were entirely inappropriate. It was vital, for her sake, to create an atmosphere of serenity and peace.

And, thank God, her death *was* peaceful. She had been terrified of choking to death – a real possibility once the cancer spread to her lungs. She also had a deep fear of being buried alive and begged me to ensure that she was completely and utterly 'gone' before any undertaker approached.

No mother expects to have such conversations with their child. At least she and I had plenty of time – at a much earlier stage, of course – to discuss the important things, including her sons' future, and to say a proper goodbye. Not all parents are so blessed. We were also lucky in that she was treated at one of the best hospitals in America, if not in the world. Indeed, for the first 13 months of her cancer, she was expected to survive. During that time, I wrote a short story about her illness and deliberately gave it a happy ending.

The story, entitled 'Worms', was prompted by my grandson Will, whom I was taking to the school-bus from his home on Mercer Island. As we walked along, we kept seeing earthworms stranded on the sidewalk and Will insisted on stopping to put each and every worm safely back into the soil. 'Worms mustn't die,' he told me, with deep feeling – not needing to spell out who *else* mustn't die.

Realizing how much worse it was for two small boys to have their mother so gravely ill helped me cope myself. With their father already dead, it was an appalling shock for them when she was first diagnosed, in November 2006, with cancer of the tongue. Tongue-cancer is extremely rare among non-smokers and the under-65s; Pauline was only 40 and had never smoked in her life. In an extra-ordinary, 7-hour operation, the surgeon cut out part of her tongue, along with the tumour; stitched skin from her forearm to the remaining piece of tongue, using a string of blood-vessels (excised from along her upper arm) like a length of sewing thread, to do the stitching. He then patched the arm with skin from her thigh, having already removed 14 lymph-nodes through an incision in the neck. The tongue-graft and the tracheotomy left her badly scarred and, later, after extensive radiation, her face was encrusted with livid red burns, and the inside of her mouth covered with bleeding blisters, which meant she had to be fed by stomach-tube.

Radiation in the mouth is one of the most brutal of cancer treatments and involves being immobilized and bolted to a table, with a claustrophobic mask fitted to one's face, neck and chest, clamped so tightly the patient cannot move a muscle. Yet, throughout the long, gruelling weeks of treatment, Pauline never indulged in self-pity, nor, later, when she lost her bounteous brown hair and had to wear a wig. Indeed, just days after the initial operation, although unable to speak, she could still write, with wry humour: 'I look like a lopsided chipmunk, with a lollipop tongue. I have a cast on my left arm and a hole in my right thigh and physically I feel like a jigsaw puzzle. The notion of putting one's foot in one's mouth takes on a whole new meaning now that my tongue is made from other parts of me!'

Her remarkable courage set me an example I draw on even now. Whatever the horrors she had to endure – severe side-effects from the high doses of narcotics; infections caused by the stomach-tube; frequent bouts of pneumonia; crops of viral mouth-ulcers; hypothyroidism; increasing weight-loss; recurrent nausea – she remained heroically positive. Despite my natural pessimism (not to mention cowardice), I knew I must be worthy of her.

My whole world had overturned when I first heard the diagnosis and dread took up residence within my home and heart. Faced with a crisis completely beyond my control, all my previous problems shrunk to pygmy-size. However, gradually and painfully, I did my poor best to be strong and that itself proved a useful coping-mechanism. Once, I had taught my daughter how to read, how to sew, how to plant nasturtiums; now she was teaching me far more important life-lessons.

When I wasn't with her in person, I tried to support her with daily or twice-daily emails. Phone calls were more difficult, not only because of the time-difference (Seattle is 8 hours behind), but because for much of the time she had no voice, or only a hoarse and whispery one, or she coughed so much it was impossible to hear her. Knowing that I myself had suffered illness, fear and loss, and at an early age, helped to reassure her that such states *are*, in fact, endurable. I also urged her to try to join, in spirit, with the millions of suffering people throughout the world, who, although strangers to each other, are united by their pain and grief. I've always found this an effective way of feeling less alone; of moving from a sense of isolation to an awareness of shared sorrow within the human family, the community at large.

I also had to persuade her to accept the limitations of her illness, which had forced her to slow down. She continually worried about her job as a freelance marketing consultant and, despite the severity of her condition, chafed to be back at work. Because she was used to cramming five lives into one, it was extremely hard for her to be bed-bound and inert. Indeed, halfway through her long and painful illness, she decided to set up as a cancer-coach, using her own experience. From her sickbed, she drew up a complex business plan, embracing every aspect of cancer-care from counselling to plastic surgery; from domestic help to advice on wigs and make-up.

Although, again, I admired her courage in this venture, I also suggested, gently, that she try to become a sloth. I emailed her photos of various different sloths – two-toed, three-toed, tree-sloths, ground sloths – along with detailed descriptions of their deliciously idle habits, which I hoped she'd emulate. I had always called her my chick, so I sent all my subsequent emails from 'Mummy-sloth' to 'sloth-chick'.

I still have all the emails – mine to her, hers to me – and also the notes she scrawled when I was with her in America, either at home or in the hospital. She communicated, when voiceless, via scribbled notes on a yellow shorthand pad. Both notes and emails form a precious record of how close we felt to each other, even when I was back in England, with an ocean and a land-mass in between. The special bond between us dates back to the early 1970s, when I was a single parent for a while: the two of us against the world. Once, we went to Butlins together – the only affordable holiday then – where she was crowned Miss Junior Princess, in a costume I created from one of my frilly petticoats, yards of lace, a cardboard tiara and an inordinate amount of glitter.

Her illness changed the nature of our bond. She could confide in me her fear of death and her doubts about – yet yearning for – an afterlife, and know I'd understand, since I had wrestled with such issues since my teens. I ached to take the cancer from her; even to die instead of her. Although that wasn't possible, it was surely more appropriate, since *she* was in her prime, with a new husband and two sons to nurture, whereas I was in my sixties. All the pain she suffered, I seemed to experience myself, as if she were still part of my own body; still an infant in the womb. I hope at least it helped her feel a little less alone, knowing we were so closely linked, in body and in mind.

I also bought her a copy of Take That's 'Royal Road', as the lyrics seemed so apt: 'Don't close your eyes . . . Don't fade away . . . Stay with me, girl . . . Don't leave me . . . ' And, from then on, all my emails bore the postscript: 'Stay with me, girl . . . Don't leave me.' She *did* fade away; *did* leave me, and I only have to hear that song to feel a sense of utter bleakness. Sometimes, I can't believe she's gone; indeed, half an hour after her death, I actually said to someone who was talking, 'Sssh! Be quiet. Don't wake her.'

However, I've discovered tangible ways of remaining close. Her husband gave me a present of her coat, as a comfort-blanket for the harrowing flight home and, although it's too long – she was taller – and navy blue (not my favourite colour), I continue to wear it now. I seem to sense her presence in the fabric; the imprint of her fingers on the buttons and, when I thrust my hands into the pockets, I can almost feel *her* hands.

The first time I put it on, I found a cent in the pocket – not quite enough, alas, to meet the high cost of her illness. In the States, you either pay or you're cast into the street, and many Americans with cancer end up bankrupt. Thus, one practical way of helping was to shoulder some of the bills – the most worthwhile money I've ever spent, because every extra month she lived meant another month with her sons. And, aware how young they were to be orphaned, her struggle was for *their* sake, first and foremost.

In their different ways, they both matched their mother's courage. Ned read to her when she was too weak to pick up a book; held cool flannels against her burning forehead, urging her, 'Be brave, Mom!' And when, in October 2007, Will put his leg through the glass in the front door and suffered horrendous cuts, he sat in stoical silence in the ambulance and throughout the painful stitching of his wounds. Yet, obviously, both boys were prey to hideous fear, and the vividness of their imaginations was frequently brought home to me. On the day of her death, Will asked, 'Is Mom a ghost now?', and, later, during a family discussion about a suitable memorial for the grave, he suddenly remarked, 'We can't plant a tree, because the roots would get tangled up with Mom's feet.'

I gave the boys my St Christopher pendant – a present from a friend in England, to protect me on the flights to Seattle. Ten hours on a plane was nothing compared with their own intractable journey from anguish to acceptance and endurance. Memories of their bravery continue to inspire me in the dark days since the death. Indeed, memories in general are an important survival-tool. I keep a sort of scrapbook in my head and it's full of Pauline, vibrantly alive: as a baby, toddler, schoolgirl, undergraduate, career-woman, hostess, bride and then mother in her turn. Even death cannot take away the fact that I enjoyed my daughter at all those different stages, and was important in her life.

Many women are less fortunate; especially those infertile, as I originally presumed myself to be. After Pauline's birth, I suffered another miscarriage but never had another living child, despite endless tests and infertility treatments. But, against all the odds, I did have *one* child – and one is infinitely, triumphantly better than none. Of course, I miss her desperately; feel sad on Mothers' Day, when there is no card or phone call or bouquet; of course, I grieve that she won't be at my deathbed, as I was at *my* mother's, and, of course, I bitterly regret all the extra years we might have had together. But regret is futile. Better far to focus on the years we *did* have. And, actually, many people have remarked that Pauline lived her life with such intensity, she achieved more in her 42 years than others do in twice that time. Her husband, Herb, used to call her his 'Bright Star' and said, as part of his funeral oration, 'Bright stars shine brilliantly, but typically a shorter time'.

What also helps is the knowledge that she is now at peace. At times, her sufferings were so extreme, I could hardly bear to witness them. On one occasion, she was given a Methadone overdose, in error. I found her lying like a junkie: body drenched in sweat and shaking uncontrollably; feet twitching, hands clawing the air, eyeballs rolling up in their sockets, mouth grimacing or muttering gobbledegook. She had no idea I was there and later described her state as a hellish one of confusion, agitation and hallucination.

Worse sufferings were to follow. In November 2007, just 5 days after celebrating a whole year free from cancer (an all-important milestone, since it greatly increased her chances of survival), we learned the devastating news that she had now developed an inoperable tumour in her lung. Slowly but inexorably, the ferocious cancer spread to her liver, pleura, blood and bones, and she had to draw on yet more reserves of courage to make preparations for her death. Besides the letters to her sons, she also left them cards and presents, to be given to them on every birthday until they reached 21. She also had photos taken of her *with* the boys, cuddling them and smiling, so they would have a vivid memento of their mother, happy and alive, and also arranged for her second husband to formally adopt them. Rather than saying 'Why me?' or 'Poor me!', she used her remaining time to ensure that she left things in good order and that her sons' loss would be eased as far as was humanly possible.

And it's the boys who help me survive. Pauline asked me to keep her memory alive and to remind them constantly of her love. The night of the actual funeral, I tucked them into bed and talked about her, long into the night. They were surrounded by a menagerie of cuddly toys – the same toys they'd left with Pauline in the hospital, during the last stage of her illness. I reminded them that because these animals had shared her bed, they would now bear her special imprint, so, if they put their faces against the creatures' fur, they would feel their mother's touch. I knew it was imperative to provide the boys with a sense of her continuing presence, and, finally, they fell asleep; Ned with his bear and lion; Will with his wolf and wolf-cub, his turtle and his anteater.

Ned and Will are part of Pauline and carry on her legacy and genes, and thus they are my lifebuoys, however weak the pun. No one could deny that the death of a child – even a grown-up child – is profoundly traumatic. My sister, who lost a son of 33, told me, a few years ago, that she re-experienced the grief every single day. It was no worse, she said, on his birthday or the anniversary of his death – it was a constant, daily, gnawing sense of loss. At the time, I didn't fully understand. Only now do I grasp the truth of her words; waking daily to the reality of having lost my daughter; wrestling nightly with gruesome images of her thin, grey, lifeless body, or the heartlessly glossy coffin that seemed to mock her own bruised and shrunken state. Just the sound of a child calling 'Mummy!' in the street, or the sight of a mother and daughter out shopping together, arm in arm, never fails to reignite the pang of loss. I'm moved to tears by every bereaved parent I see on television; by every soldier in Afghanistan, cut down in his prime. Yet the existence of all those other unchilded parents stops me railing at cruel fate. Just as Pauline never said 'Why me?', I avoid it, too. As simply one of a whole throng of grieving mothers, why feel myself singled out?

My greatest consolation is that I had my child for 42 years – 42 years longer than was predicted at the outset. Another inestimable blessing was the fact that, throughout her illness, she was surrounded by exceptional people. Chief of these was her husband, who matched her own heroism by his unselfish and unwavering devotion, and whose grown-up children, Breanne and Cameron, were also profoundly caring, and continue even now to act like a set of extra parents – although more fun because they're young. And Pauline's father, Tim, lent new meaning to the cliché, 'a tower of strength'. Pauline called it a 'wonderful gift' to have grown so close to her father during the long period of her illness and to talk with him about intimate subjects, previously off-limits. And his new wife, Angela, was equally devoted in the sheer time and care she poured out on my daughter.

Deep pain can forge deep bonds; intense grief creates intense friendships. Angela and I are much closer than we ever were before. Far from feeling like the supplanted ex-wife, I derived huge comfort from her presence and from her unstinting help and support, and we've kept in touch ever since. It's no longer a question of being united in suffering with a community of strangers, but with a community of family and friends. Pauline's friends are now *my* friends and it helped ease my pain to be 'Mom' to them, as well, when, after her death, they clung to me and sobbed.

One couple in particular – Kay Diamond and Wahaab Baldwin – were described by Pauline as 'two of the most special people on the planet'. She even appointed them as her son's official guardians, if – God forbid – Herb, too, should die. Wahaab, a Christian Sufi minister, presided at both Pauline's wedding and at her funeral, and he and Kay provided every possible help – emotional, spiritual and physical – throughout the 2 years of her illness. They also set up the Pauline Patrol: a group of friends and neighbours, who pledged to help the family with cooking, chauffeuring, hospital-visiting, or arranging play-dates for the boys. After Pauline's death, their support continued, although the ladies of the group renamed themselves Herb's Harem!

These remarkable people deepened my understanding of what love really means. Far from seeming put upon or burdened, they performed their countless services with alacrity, affection, serenity and selflessness. If I want my mood to lift, I only have to remember all their kindnesses: Teri, Lorraine and the two Susans calling in on mercy-missions, to bring food or help or comfort; Kay, busy in the kitchen, pureeing beets and spinach, to enhance the standard mix-ture in Pauline's feeding-tube; Teresa and Rodney taking the boys home for sleepovers – supper, breakfast, help with homework, all thrown in, as well; the kindly bus-driver refusing to accept my fare on the daily journey to the hospital. 'If your daughter's sick, you ride free,' he declared. 'And my wife and I are praying for her, you know.' Such sheer good will gave Pauline's illness a rare redemptory aspect – unexpected, and consoling.

One of Pauline's closest friends, Beth Baska, even provided me with an outfit for the funeral, buying a range of clothes on approval, so I could choose one that fitted well. When I flew out in August 2008, Pauline was in sudden, miraculous remission, so all I'd packed was casual gear, suitable for playing with kids and walking dogs.

While I was on the plane, she suffered a pulmonary haemorrhage and was rushed back into hospital. Beth was there to meet me at the airport; to break the tragic news and drive me full-pelt to my daughter's side.

Later, and despite my protests, she refused to take a single cent for my smart black trouser-suit. She said Pauline had been 'her inspiration', and emailed me on the first anniversary of the death: 'I still miss her terribly, but I know she'd want me to stop feeling sorry for myself and get out there and make a difference.' And that's it – in a nutshell. My brave and upbeat daughter would certainly hate the thought of us indulging in self-pity, rather than getting on with life.

She knew, from her own experience of bereavement, that keeping busy is highly therapeutic. During her illness, I had already planned a new novel, again about a daughter with cancer and again with a happy ending. After her death, I removed the cancer theme and changed the plot entirely, but I continued writing the book in her memory, finding the process therapeutic, in that it gave me discipline and focus when I was in danger of falling apart. Occasionally, I even sensed she was helping me from some mysterious realm beyond the grave and, by tuning in to this 'help', I'd feel a little less bereft. The novel is called *Broken Places*, from a line in Hemingway's *A Farewell To Arms*: 'the world breaks everyone and, afterward, many are strong at the broken places'. This was relevant not just to the book, but to all of us who, broken by Pauline's death – yet inspired by her example – have gone on to be stronger.

I'd like to finish with two different quotations, in the hope they may provide some solace to other grieving parents. Firstly, the lines my sister, Lorna, sent me on New Year's Eve 2008, which would have been Pauline's forty-third birthday and is also the anniversary of the death of Nigel, Lorna's eldest son: 'The life of one we loved is never lost. Its influence goes on through all the lives it ever touched.'

Both Nigel and Pauline's lives touched many people and, we, the survivors, keep the two cousins alive in our different ways and through our different memories. Every New Year's Eve, my sister and I light candles for our children and put flowers in front of their photographs – another healing ritual. Candles are a symbol not just of light in darkness but of the uncertainty of life all too easily extinguished, and thus are doubly appropriate.

My second quotation is the poem that Pauline's father read at her memorial service – a poem that reflects her own buoyant, life-affirming spirit:

You can shed tears that she has gone,
Or you can smile because she has lived.
You can close your eyes and pray that she will come back,
Or you can open your eyes and see all that she has left us.
Your heart can be empty because you cannot see her,
Or you can be full of the love you shared.
You can turn your back on tomorrow and live yesterday,
Or you can be happy for tomorrow because of yesterday.
You can remember her, and only that she has gone,
Or you can cherish her memory and let it live on.
You can cry and close your mind, be empty and turn back,
Or you can do what she would want:
Open your eyes, love and go on.

# Afterword
## Dorothy Rowe

*Dorothy Rowe is a world renowned clinical psychologist and writer. Born in Australia, she has a grown-up son and is now based in Britain where she has worked extensively for the National Health Service. She is the author of 15 books, including* Depression: The Way Out of Your Prison *and, most recently,* Why We Lie.

The Australian psychologist and writer Andee Jones was worried about her son, a lovely young man who had lost his way. Later, when writing about how she learnt of his suicide, she said,

I've been floating in a paper boat on an ice-black sea. There's a blood-curdling crack! And the massive shelf crashes down, plunging me into the glacial deep, tearing me to shreds with its scalpels. The giant shards rip through me, freezing blood, guts, lungs and brain. Am I dead? How can I not be dead? If I'm not dead, let me wake up from this nightmare.[1]

A year later, she wrote that

the knife is still embedded in my heart. . . . I don't know how to go on. Being alive and awake is the stomach-sinking, palpitating experience of sitting in a hospital cubicle waiting for test results. Don't get dressed yet, dear, we might need to get you straight into theatre.[2]

Each in his or her own way, the authors of these chapters have lived through what Andee Jones experienced. They have learned that, when someone dear to us dies, our whole being and our world shatters and falls into a kind of painful nothingness. Grief, as C. S. Lewis said, 'feels like fear'. Indeed, grief is fear, the fear that your whole sense of being a person and your world has fallen apart, even disappeared. You have become a non-person in a non-world.

Yet you have to move and act as if the world that other people know is still there, and that you are the person you have always been, only now you are sad. Other people do not see that loss and grief have turned you into a ghost in your own life.

Few people understand that what each of us knows as myself and my world, what we call 'I', 'me', 'myself', is made up all the ideas, hopes, dreams, images that have formed in our brain and mind during our existence. The person you love is an important part of that structure. When that person dies, part of the structure that is you is torn away. What is left shakes and threatens to fall apart.

However, there is always enough left to be the observer of what is happening and say, 'I feel I am falling apart'. The structure that is you rebuilds itself, but it can never be what it once was. From then on a sense of absence is always part of who you are.

Some people die of grief but most do not. They learn how to keep the broken structure of themselves hidden from those who do not want to see that grief is ugly and disturbing, just as Picasso showed in his portrait of a woman grieving. Nor do they want to be reminded that to love is always to risk loss. The platitudinous lies that other people tell, that 'time heals' and how important it is to seek 'closure' so you 'can get on with your life', force those grieving to hide their grief and pretend that they are 'taking it well'. They might give the appearance of leading a normal life, but they know that the one who has been lost can never be replaced, and that they will live with their grief forever.

For such a loss there is no recompense, no reward. All that those in grief can do is to do what all of us can do when we are trapped in a painful situation from which there is no escape. We can re-construe it, that is, we give it a different meaning, something with which we hope we can live. However, the death of someone we love never allows us to construct a meaning in which there is no pain. No meaning, however comforting, can ever replace what might have been. As time passes the pain becomes softer but never disappears completely.

Even when the person who dies is very old and suffering great pain, or has enormous physical disabilities for which there is no cure or amelioration, being told that the death is a 'merciful release' is not a comfort because, even if the person is beyond pain, you are not. You have to bear the pain of that loss and all that that loss means to you.

Each of us has the task of surviving both physically and as a person. We are born with a very keen sense of what might be a threat to us, and with a very readily activated defence, that of anger. Anger is an emotion that carries the meaning, 'How dare that happen to me!' (All emotions are meanings where the subject is always the person feeling the emotion.) The death of someone we love is a threat to our sense of being a person. Consequently we cannot help but be angry.

Wise people know how important it is to acknowledge our anger. Unacknowledged anger does not dissipate but stays inside us, only to make itself felt when we least expect it. Unfortunately, many of us are taught as children that our anger is unacceptable, even wicked. We bury our anger and thus fail to learn how to express it in a multitude of socially acceptable but self-affirming ways.

When our anger does make itself felt, we do not know what to do with it. Some people believe that, if they give vent to their anger, they will be completely rejected by other people. They are so frightened of being punished in this way for being angry that they refuse to recognize their anger as anger, and instead call it fear. They then find a cause for their fear somewhere in the world around them and refuse to leave the safety of their homes.

Some people who have been bereaved react in this way. Robin Baird-Smith tells in his essay how, when he relaxed his guard, he was surprised to feel an anger so fierce that his whole body shook. He recognized that the meaning, 'How dare this happen to me!' demands having someone to blame. However, Robin was reluctant to respond in this way. He had been busy removing any likely object for his anger out of harm's way. He writes: 'How could I feel angry with the driver who had driven into me? I learned subsequently that his girlfriend who was in the passenger seat has suffered far worse and longer lasting orthopaedic injuries than me.' Robin could not allow himself that complexity of thought of which we are all capable where we tolerate two conflicting emotions.

It is possible to feel sympathy for the person who has injured us while, occasionally, experiencing intense anger, even to the point of wishing to kill that person. It is possible to express this wish, not by putting it into action, but by imagining ourselves doing what we wish to do. Children who are allowed to daydream quickly discover the advantages of lying in bed and imagining severe punishments for their mother who had spoken to them sharply and sent them to bed, but then finding in the morning that not only they are no longer angry with her, but she is there to get their breakfast.

By expressing our anger in imagination we can, eventually, dissipate it. In the space of time that we feel an emotion, that emotion is our own truth. We need always to acknowledge our own truths, and not deny them or pretend they are different from what they are. Children learn, not so much from what their parents tell them, but from what their parents do. If, in times of high emotion, parents do not explain to their children what they are doing, their children have to make their own interpretations.

Afterword

Children need to be shown that all emotions are naturally self-limiting. Falling in love might come to an end, or it might transmute into that softer emotion of love that can last a lifetime. Mummy and Daddy might sometimes be angry with one another and argue, but their anger is soon over while their love for each other goes on forever.

The meaning, 'How dare this happen to me', gives our sense of being a person a certain coherence while grief shatters it. Not knowing what to do, some parents hide their grief from their children. Adults protect themselves from a child's grief by telling themselves that it is best if children are not told about a sibling's or a parent's death because 'children soon forget'. These fail to understand that children are human beings like themselves, and that we do not forget events for which we have been given no satisfactory explanation. We continue to puzzle over these events, and often arrive at conclusions that worry us much more than the truth would have done.

Anyone who doubts that children, however young, should be told that someone close to them has died should read Louise Patten's essay about the death of her brother Charles. When he became ill, as her older sister Anne-Marie recalled, the adults in the family slipped into 'a state of Paglossian denial'. 'Denial' is a word that we psychotherapists use because we prefer to use soft-sounding 'expert' words instead of the words that everyone can use. To deny that something that does exist does not is to lie. Anne-Marie learned from people outside the family that Charles was dying. When she questioned what her parents had told her, she was sent away from home. Louise wanted to believe her parents but she could hear Charles screaming in pain. She was sure that Charles wanted her to comfort him, but her parents forbade her to go to his room because she was 'too noisy'. She did not believe them.

When we discover that someone has lied to us about something important we never fully trust that person again. No one explained to the children why Charles suddenly vanished into hospital. Then they were told that he had gone to heaven. They were not allowed to go to his funeral, and no one mentioned the word 'death'. Even when we watch someone die, we can find it hard to believe that the person is no more. When all we have been given is a report of the death of someone important to us, it can take us a very long time to accept that the report is true. Louise was sure that her parents were mistaken. Charles was alive and would be home for Christmas.

On the day that Wendy Perriam's daughter Pauline died, leaving two sons, Will and Ned, Will asked Wendy, 'Is Mom a ghost now?', and later, during a family discussion about a suitable memorial for the grave, he suddenly remarked, 'We can't plant a tree, because the roots would get tangled up with Mom's feet'. This was a family where the children's grief was acknowledged and they were given help to deal with it. I marvelled at Wendy's strength in being able to do what she did in the midst of her own grief, but her understanding of people that we see in her novels is such that she could not have done otherwise.

Children who are not told the truth about a death in the family often blame themselves for that death. Unless an adult explains to them that they are not to blame, the guilt that these children feel is likely to have deleterious effects throughout the children's lives. Often as adults, people cannot understand why their life has gone so wrong, but they cannot seek an answer by examining their childhood because they believe that it is wrong to blame their parents for what had happened in their childhood.

So prevalent is this belief that, in describing how her parents excluded her and her siblings from everything to do with the death of her little sister Clare, Joanna Moorhead feels obliged to explain,

'What seemed best to them was to make life as normal as possible: and in that, I believe, they were right'. However, we cannot increase our understanding of ourselves if we think solely in terms of good and bad, blame, guilt and punishment.

We need to understand that what determines our behaviour is not what happens to us but how we interpret what happens to us. Our interpretations can come from only one place, what we know at the time.

As adults we should look at our childhood in two ways, how we interpret childhood events now, and how we interpreted them at the time. Children make the best interpretations they can, given what they know at the time. Often they are wiser and more truthful than the adults around them.

The interpretations we create always have consequences. The consequences of how you as a child interpreted events form part of who you are today. We need to remember, not only how we as children interpreted events, but why we chose certain interpretations rather than others. Looking back like this, with our two perspectives at the loss of someone we love, we might discover the grief that we were not allowed to express and the anger that we had to bury. Acknowledging our grief and anger, even much later in our life, can help us reduce the pain of our loss.

People whose thinking about themselves is always within the framework of blame and guilt often become experts in feeling guilty. When they ask themselves, 'Who is to blame for my loss?', their immediate answer is themselves. They soon discover that blaming themselves for their loss is, in fact, the recipe for turning natural sadness into depression[3]

Depression has many purposes. It is a way, albeit a very painful way, of holding yourself together when you feel that you are falling apart. Depression gives you the space and time to put yourself back together in a different, wiser way. Depression is a means of avoiding the chaos in your life, and of avoiding some painful truths. One of these painful truths is that, while we like to think that we have our life under control, we live in a world where things happen by chance. We are always at the mercy of events. Many of us find such helplessness intolerable, and choose instead to feel guilty for not having prevented a disaster.

Feeling guilty for having acted or failed to act carries within it the meaning, 'I was in control of the situation and could have acted differently had I chosen to do so'. In the absence of any evidence that you were in control of the situation and could have prevented the disaster, feeling guilty acts as a defence against the fear of feeling helpless. Feeling guilty to defend against the fear of being helpless is a terrible waste of time and effort, as is being depressed. Lost in such guilt or depression, we are so completely taken up with ourselves that we ignore other people. Yet, it is from other people that we might learn how to accept and live with our helplessness, and how to share the burden of the grief that everyone carries.

We all suffer loss. No one escapes. We can also learn that, when we love someone, our image of that person makes a home inside us, and in its own way comforts and guides us until the day we die. Each of the chapters in this book is about the image of the person the writer loved and has never entirely lost.

### Notes

1 Andee Jones, *Barking Mad: Too Much Therapy Is Never Enough* (Publish In Ink, 2010), p.159.
2 Ibid., p. 198.
3 See Dorothy Rowe, *Depression: The Way Out of Your Prison*, 3rd ed. (Routledge, 2003).

# 'Sad is a place'

## Michael Rosen

Sad is a place
that is deep and dark
like the space
under the bed

Sad is a place
that is high and light
like the sky
above my head

When it's deep and dark
I don't dare to go there

When it's high and light
I want to be thin air.

*From* Michael Rosen's Sad Book ©*Michael Rosen, published in 2004 after the death from meningitis of his 19-year-old son Eddie. Reproduced by permission of Walker Books Ltd, London SE 11 5HJ.*

# Glossary of Useful Organizations

**ACT** is a UK-wide charity working to achieve the best possible quality of life and care for every child and young person who is not expected to reach adulthood. It supports youngsters and their families. www.act.org.uk or call 0845 108 2201.

**Brake**, the road safety charity, works with those who have been injured in road accidents and those who have lost loved ones. www brake.org.uk or call its victims and carers helpline on 0845 6038570.

**Care for the Family** is a national charity which aims to promote strong family life and to help those who face family difficulties, including the loss of a child. Its motivation is Christian compassion. Call 029 2081 0800 or www.careforthefamily.org.uk.

**The Child Bereavement Charity** supports families and educates professionals both when a child dies and when a child is bereaved. Every year the charity trains around 5000 professionals across health care, social care, education, the emergency services and the voluntary sector. It also provides a support and information service (01494 568900), award-winning resources, an interactive website with online forums, and a Buckinghamshire-based family bereavement support service. It can be contacted at www.childbereavement.org.uk.

**The Child Death Helpline** is a helpline for anyone affected by the death of a child of any age, from prebirth to adult, under any circumstances, however recently or long ago. It is manned by volunteers, all of them bereaved parents, and is run as a partnership between professionals and parents. The helpline number is 0800 282986 and they can be contacted at www.childdeathhelpline.org.uk.

**The Compassionate Friends** is a charitable organization of bereaved parents, siblings and grandparents dedicated to the support and care of other bereaved parents, siblings, and grandparents who have suffered the death of a child. It has a national helpline (0845 1232304) and offers support both directly to bereaved families and indirectly by fostering understanding and good practice amongst professionals concerned with child death and by increasing public awareness. It can be contacted at 53 North Street, Bristol, BS3 1EN or at www.tcf.org.uk.

**Cruse Bereavement Care**, the UK's biggest bereavement charity, offers a telephone helpline (0844 477 9400) and face-to-face support and practical advice from trained volunteer counsellors via its branch network. It also has a special website for bereaved youngsters which can be accessed via its main website www.crusebereavementcare. org.uk.

**The Foundation for the Study of Infant Deaths** (**FSID**) works to prevent sudden infant deaths by funding research. It also supports bereaved families. www.fsid.org.uk or 0808 802 6868.

**If I Should Die** is a website which provides practical, non-denominational information to all those facing bereavement. www. ifishoulddie.co.uk.

**The Miscarriage Association** supports those who have suffered miscarriages, ectopic and molar pregnancies. www.miscarriageassociation. org.uk or 01924 200799.

**The Jimmy Mizen Foundation**, set up by Barry and Margaret Mizen, and their children, after the death of their son Jimmy (as described in Barry's essay), works to encourage young people to play a positive role in society. www.jimmymizen.org or 0845 272 5262.

**The Stillbirth and Neonatal Death Society (Sands)** offers support to anyone affected by the death of a baby and works in partnership with health professionals to improve the quality of care and services offered to bereaved families. www.uk-sands.org or 020 7436 5881.

**The James Wentworth-Stanley Memorial Fund** was set up by a mother whose 21-year-old son took his own life. It aims to raise awareness of the causes of suicide in the young and promote research. www.jwsmf.org.

## DATE DUE

| | | | |
|---|---|---|---|
| | | | |
| | | | |
| | | | |
| | | | |
| | | | |
| | | | |
| | | | |
| | | | |
| | | | |
| | | | |
| | | | |
| | | | |
| | | | |
| | | | |
| | | | |
| | | | |
| | | | |
| | | | |
| | | | |
| | | | |
| | | | |
| GAYLORD | | | PRINTED IN U.S.A. |